Michael J.C. Gordon

THE DENOTATIONAL DESCRIPTION OF PROGRAMMING LANGUAGES

An Introduction

Springer-Verlag
New York Heidelberg Berlin

Michael J. C. Gordon
Computer Laboratory
University of Cambridge
Corn Exchange Street
Cambridge CB2 3QG
Great Britain

AMS Subject Classifications (1970): 68-A30

Library of Congress Cataloging in Publication Data

Gordon, Michael J C 1948–
The denotational description of programming languages.

Bibliography: p.
Includes indexes.
1. Programming languages (Electronic computers)
I. Title.
QA76.7.G67 001.6′424 79-15723

Printed in the United States of America.

9 8 7 6 5 4 3
Third Printing 1984

ISBN 0-387-90433-6 Springer-Verlag New York Heidelberg Berlin
ISBN 3-540-90433-6 Springer-Verlag Berlin Heidelberg New York

Preface

This book explains how to formally describe programming languages using the techniques of *denotational semantics*. The presentation is designed primarily for computer science students rather than for (say) mathematicians. *No* knowledge of the theory of computation is required, but it would help to have some acquaintance with high level programming languages. The selection of material is based on an undergraduate semantics course taught at Edinburgh University for the last few years. Enough descriptive techniques are covered to handle all of ALGOL 60, PASCAL and other similar languages.

Denotational semantics combines a powerful and lucid descriptive notation (due mainly to Strachey) with an elegant and rigorous theory (due to Scott). This book provides an introduction to the descriptive techniques without going into the background mathematics at all. In some ways this is very unsatisfactory; reliable reasoning about semantics (e.g. correctness proofs) cannot be done without knowing the underlying model and so learning semantic notation without its model theory could be argued to be pointless. My own feeling is that there is plenty to be gained from acquiring a purely intuitive understanding of semantic concepts together with manipulative competence in the notation, for these equip one with a powerful conceptual framework—a framework enabling one to visualize languages and constructs in an elegant and machine-independent way. Perhaps a good analogy is with calculus: for many practical purposes (e.g. engineering calculations) an intuitive understanding of how to differentiate and integrate is all that is needed. Once the utility of the ideas and techniques are appreciated it becomes much easier to motivate the underlying mathematical notions (like limits and continuity). Similarly an intuitive understanding of the descriptive techniques of denotational semantics is valuable, both as a tool for understanding programming, and as a motivation for the advanced theory.

Because the underlying mathematics is not described I have occasionally used notation which, whilst intuitively straightforward, is technically sloppy. For example I have used the symbol = with several conceptually similar, but mathematically distinct, meanings. I felt it best not to introduce minor technical distinctions and restrictions if they could not be satisfactorily explained. Any reader familiar with Scott's theory should easily be able to detect and correct the few abuses of notation.

I have changed certain standard notations to be less standard but more mnemonic. Also, since one or two standard symbols were not available on the typesetting machine used, I have had to use substitutes. I hope the overall attractiveness of the typesetting compensates for the slightly unorthodox appearance of some of the notation.

Acknowledgements

None of the material in this book is original; that which has not been published is part of the folklore of the subject. In deciding how to present things I was strongly influenced by Milne and Strachey's advanced treatise [Milne & Strachey]. Jim Donahue, Robert Milne and Bob Tennent all made detailed criticisms of an early draft—I have tried to implement their suggestions as much as possible. Errors in the final draft were pointed out to me by members of CS4 and the postgraduate theory course (78/79); special thanks to: Gordon Brebner, Mark Jerrum, Alan Mycroft, Don Sanella and Michael Sanderson. Finally I'd like to thank the following people for numerous fruitful discussions, suggestions and explanations: Dana Angluin, Rod Burstall, Avra Cohn, Dave Macqueen, Robin Milner, Peter Mosses, Mogens Nielsen, Gordon Plotkin, Jerry Schwarz and Chris Wadsworth.

The writing of this book was supported by the Science Research Council.

Many people have drawn my attention to errors in the first printing, particularly Roberto Bigonha of U.C.L.A. and Simon of the University of Exeter.

Contents

Contents

Contents

Contents

Introduction

1. Introduction

1.1. Syntax, semantics and pragmatics

The study of a natural or artificial language is traditionally split into three areas:

(i) Syntax: This deals with the form, shape, structure etc. of the various expressions in the language.
(ii) Semantics: This deals with the meaning of the language.
(iii) Pragmatics: This deals with the uses of the language.

For programming languages the words "syntax" and "semantics" both have fairly clear meanings; "pragmatics" on the other hand is rather more vague—some people use the term to cover anything to do with implementations (the idea being that languages are 'used' via implementations); others use the term for the study of the 'practical value' of programming concepts. We shall discuss our uses of "syntax" and "semantics" later in the book; the word "pragmatics" will be avoided.

1.2. The purposes of formal semantics

This book is about the *formal* semantics of programming languages. The word "formal" means that our study will be based on precise mathematical principles (although we shall avoid the actual mathematics). Many books on programming languages discuss meanings *intuitively* or *informally*. For example in the PASCAL report [Jensen and Wirth] the meaning of an assignment statement is described thus: "The assignment statement serves to replace the current value of a variable by a new value specified as an expression". For many purposes this is a perfectly adequate semantic description and one might wonder if there is any point in being more formal. To see that there is, we now briefly discuss three uses of formal techniques:

(i) Providing precise machine-independent concepts.
(ii) Providing unambiguous specification techniques.
(iii) Providing a rigorous theory to support reliable reasoning.

We shall explain each of these in turn.

1.2.1. Providing precise and machine-independent concepts

When informally describing or comparing languages one frequently makes use of various concepts. For example, recall the description of the PASCAL assignment statement quoted above. If one were trying to explain this to someone who knew nothing about programming one would have to explain:

(i) The concept of a "variable".
(ii) What the "current value" of a variable is.
(iii) How a value is "specified as an expression".

One way of explaining these would be to describe some actual implementation of PASCAL [say the one for the DEC 10 computer] and then to explain how variables, current values, expression evaluation, etc., are represented. The trouble with this is that if someone else had been given explanations with respect to a different implementation (say the one for the CDC 6000 computer) then the two explanations might assign subtly different meanings to the same concepts. In any case the "essence" of these notions clearly is not dependent on any particular machine. What a formal semantics gives one is a *universal* set of concepts, defined in terms of abstract mathematical entities, which enable things like (i), (ii), (iii) above to be explained without reference to the arbitrary mechanisms of particular implementations.

Unfortunately it is rather hard to justify the analytic power of formal concepts before the concepts themselves have been described. As we proceed the reader must decide for himself whether we are really, as claimed, providing powerful tools for thought.

1.2.2. Providing unambiguous specification techniques

Both users and implementers of a programming language need a description that is comprehensible, unambiguous and complete. During the last twenty years or so notations such as Backus-Naur form (BNF for short), supported by the concepts of formal language theory, have provided adequate ways of specifying, and thinking about, the syntax of languages. Unfortunately the development of notations and concepts for dealing with semantics has been much slower. Almost all languages have been defined in English. Although these descriptions are frequently masterpieces of apparent clarity they have nevertheless usually suffered from both inconsistency and incompleteness. For example, many different interpretations were compatible with the defining reports of both ALGOL 60 [Knuth '67] and PASCAL [Welsh, Sneeringer and Hoare]. Experience has shown that it just is not possible to achieve the necessary precision using informal descriptions.

Another reason why formal semantic definitions are useful is that they can be made machine-readable. This enables useful software tools to be produced—just as formal syntactic notations lead to tools such as parser generators. For example, Peter Mosses has produced a system which generates test-bed implementations of programming languages from formal specifications similar to those described in this book [Mosses].

1.2.3. Providing a rigorous theory to support reliable reasoning

Formal semantic techniques enable us to state and rigorously prove various properties of programs and programming languages. For example, in order to prove a program correct one must show that its actual meaning coincides with its intended meaning, and to do this both meanings must be formalised.

When reasoning about programs one is often tempted to use various apparently plausible rules of inference. For example, suppose at some point in a computation some sentence, S[**E**] involving the expression **E**, is true; then after doing the assignment **x**: = **E** one would expect S[**x**] to hold (since **x** now has the value of **E**). Thus if "**y** is prime" is true before doing the assignment **x**: = **y** then "**x** is prime" is true after it (here **E** is **y** and S[**E**] is "**E** is prime"). Although at first sight this rule seems to be intuitively correct it does not work for most real languages. For example, in PASCAL, if **x** is of type real and **y** of type integer then if the sentence "**y** is an integer" is true before doing **x**: = **y** the sentence "**x** is an integer" is *not* true after it (since the value of **y** will have been coerced to a value of type real before being assigned to **x**). It has been shown [Ligler] that for ALGOL 60 the assignment rule discussed above can fail to hold in six ways.

A formal semantics provides tools for discovering and proving exactly when rules like the above one work; without a formal semantics one has to rely on intuition—experience shows this is not enough. For example, the designers of EUCLID hoped that by making the language clean and simple the validity of various rules of inference would be intuitively obvious. Unfortunately when they came to actually write down the rules they found their correctness was not at all obvious and in the paper describing them [London *et al.*] they have to point out that they are still not sure the rules are all correct. If EUCLID had been given a formal semantics (of the type to be described in this book) then whether or not a given rule was correct would have been a matter of routine mathematical calculation.

In this book we shall concentrate on the topics discussed in 1.2.1. and 1.2.2.—readers interested in the underlying mathematics (and its use for rigorous reasoning) are advised to look at Joe Stoy's excellent text [Stoy].

1.3. Denotational semantics

The kind of formal semantics described in this book is called *denotational semantics*. The word "denotational" is used because in this approach language constructs are described by giving them *denotations*—these are abstract mathematical entities which model their meaning. We shall be going into great detail about what these denotations are and how they are related to the constructs that denote them—for the time being perhaps a hint of the idea can be conveyed by saying that the expressions **(4+2)**, **(12-6)** and **(2×3)** all denote the same number, namely the number denoted by **6**.

In the early days of the subject denotational semantics was called "mathematical semantics"—this term has now been abandoned since it incorrectly suggests that other kinds of semantics are non-mathematical. These other kinds of semantics—for example *operational semantics, axiomatic semantics* and *algebraic semantics*—are not alternative ways of doing what denotational semantics does; they each have their own set of goals. A certain amount of confusion has arisen from considering these kinds of semantics to be rival theories. This confusion leads one to undertake the useless activity of trying to decide which kind is best. To try and decide, for example, whether denotational semantics is better than axiomatic semantics is like trying to decide whether physical chemistry is better than organic chemistry.

The purposes of the various kinds of semantics are outlined below:

Denotational semantics

This is concerned with designing denotations for constructs. In this book we shall only describe denotations which model abstract machine-independent meanings; however denotations can be (and have been) designed to model particular implementations (for examples see Vol. II of [Milne and Strachey]).

Operational semantics
This is concerned with the operations of machines which run programs—namely implementations. These operations can be described with machine-oriented denotations or using non-denotational techniques like automata theory.

Axiomatic semantics
This is concerned with axioms and rules of inference for reasoning about programs.

Algebraic semantics
This is a branch of denotational semantics making use of algebraic concepts.

1.4. Abstract entities and their description

Denotational semantics is concerned with denotations—abstract entities which model meanings. Now unfortunately such abstract entities are rather elusive—indeed it is impossible to discuss them without using some particular concrete notation. For example the only way to talk about numbers is to use some arbitrary set of names like **1, 2, 3** or **I, II, III** or **one, two, three** . . . etc. Since we can not *directly* manipulate abstract entities but only talk about them with languages, perhaps we should conclude that the languages are the only things that 'really exist'.

In this book we shall write as though abstract entities like numbers or sets really do exist and that they are different from the notations and languages used to talk about them. This approach is the standard one and (we believe) leads to clean and well-structured thinking—for example, it focuses one on the 'real problems' and prevents one's thoughts from getting bogged down in inessential details (like whether to use **1, 2, 3** or **I, II, III**—there is *one* set of numbers but many ways of naming them). However it is possible to use the notation of denotational semantics whilst denying that this notation refers to abstract entities at all. If one adopts this attitude, then a denotational description is thought of as specifying a translation from one language (the language being described) to another language (a *'metalanguage'* consisting of the notations described in this book). The problem with this view is that the metalanguage—the 'target-language' of the translation—is ad hoc and not really properly defined. Now it is possible to formalize the metalanguage (see [Mosses]) but doing this, although very valuable for some purposes, is a separate task from our main goal—namely, describing programming languages—just as formalizing the language of physics is a separate task from actually doing physics (the former activity is part of the philosophy of science).

Just as mathematicians use ad hoc pieces of notation to increase clarity, so we use various informal abbreviations to make the descriptions of denotations clearer. If one thinks of semantics as being about abstract concepts then this is a natural and reasonable thing to do—the concepts are what really matter, and the notation is just one of many possible ways of talking about them. If, on the other hand, one thinks of semantics as explaining meanings by translating them into a metalanguage, then one will (rightfully) worry about the lack of precise details (for example exact syntax) of this metalanguage. For readers inclined toward the second view, this book is likely to be frustrating and unsatisfactory.

2. A first example: the language TINY

In this chapter we shall describe the syntax and semantics of a little programming language called TINY. Our purpose is to provide a vehicle for illustrating various formal concepts in use. In subsequent chapters we shall describe these concepts systematically, but here we just sketch out the main ideas and associated techniques.

2.1. Informal syntax of TINY

TINY has two main kinds of constructs, *expressions* and *commands*, both of which can contain *identifiers* which are strings of letters or digits beginning with a letter (for example **x, y1, thisisaverylongidentifier**). If we let $\mathbf{I}$, $\mathbf{I}_1$, $\mathbf{I}_2$, . . . stand for arbitrary identifiers, $\mathbf{E}$, $\mathbf{E}_1$, $\mathbf{E}_2$, . . . stand for arbitrary expressions and $\mathbf{C}$, $\mathbf{C}_1$, $\mathbf{C}_2$, . . . stand for arbitrary commands, then the constructs of TINY can be listed as follows:

$$\mathbf{E}::=\mathbf{0}\mid\mathbf{1}\mid\mathbf{true}\mid\mathbf{false}\mid\mathbf{read}\mid\mathbf{I}\mid\mathbf{not}\ \mathbf{E}\mid\mathbf{E}_1=\mathbf{E}_2\mid\mathbf{E}_1+\mathbf{E}_2$$
$$\mathbf{C}::=\mathbf{I}:=\mathbf{E}\mid\mathbf{output}\ \mathbf{E}\mid\mathbf{if}\ \mathbf{E}\ \mathbf{then}\ \mathbf{C}_1\ \mathbf{else}\ \mathbf{C}_2\mid\mathbf{while}\ \mathbf{E}\ \mathbf{do}\ \mathbf{C}\mid\mathbf{C}_1;\mathbf{C}_2$$

This notation is a variant of BNF; the symbol "$::=$" should be read as "can be" and the symbol "|" as "or". Thus a command **C** can be $\mathbf{I}:=\mathbf{E}$ or **output E** or **if E then $\mathbf{C}_1$ else $\mathbf{C}_2$** or **while E do C** or $\mathbf{C}_1;\mathbf{C}_2$. Notice that this syntactic description is ambiguous—for example it does not say whether **while E do $\mathbf{C}_1;\mathbf{C}_2$** is **(while E do $\mathbf{C}_1$);$\mathbf{C}_2$** or **while E do ($\mathbf{C}_1;\mathbf{C}_2$)**. We shall use brackets (as above) and indentation to avoid such ambiguities. In the next chapter we shall clarify further our approach to syntax.

2.2 Informal semantics of TINY

Each command of TINY, when executed, changes the *state*. This state has three components:

(i) The *memory*: this is a correspondence between identifiers and *values*. In the memory each identifier is either *bound* to some value or *unbound*.

(ii) The *input*: this is supplied by the user before programs are run; it consists of a (possibly empty) sequence of values which can be read using the expression **read** (explained later).

(iii) The *output*: this is an initially empty sequence of values which records the results of the command **output E** (explained later).

Each expression of TINY specifies a value; since expressions may contain identifiers (for example **x + y**) this value depends on the state. All values—the values of expressions, the values bound to identifiers or the values in the input or output—are either truth values (**true**, **false**) or numbers (**0,1,2,...**).

We shall now explain informally the meaning of each construct.

2.2.1. Informal semantics of expressions

The value of each expression is as follows:

(E1) **0** or **1**

The value of **0** is the number **0** and the value of **1** is the number **1**.

(E2) **true** or **false**

The value of **true** is the truth value **true** and the value of **false** is the truth value **false**.

(E3) **read**

The value of **read** is the next item on the input (an error occurs if the input is empty). **read** has the 'side effect' of removing the first item, so after it has been evaluated the input is one item shorter.

(E4) **I**

The value of an expression **I** is the value bound to **I** in the memory (if **I** is unbound an error occurs).

(E5) **not E**

If the value of **E** is **true** then the value of **not E** is **false**; if the value of **E** is **false** then the value of **not E** is **true**. In all other cases an error occurs.

(E6) $\mathbf{E_1 = E_2}$

The value of $\mathbf{E_1 = E_2}$ is **true** if the value of $\mathbf{E_1}$ equals the value of $\mathbf{E_2}$, otherwise it is **false**.

(E7) $\mathbf{E_1 + E_2}$

The value of $\mathbf{E_1 + E_2}$ is the numerical sum of the values of $\mathbf{E_1}$ and $\mathbf{E_2}$ (if either of these values is not a number then an error occurs).

2.2.2. Informal semantics of commands

(C1) **I: = E**

I is bound to the value of **E** in the memory (overwriting whatever was previously bound to **I**).

(C2) **output E**

The value of **E** is put onto the output.

(C3) **if E then $\mathbf{C_1}$ else $\mathbf{C_2}$**

If the value of **E** is **true** then $\mathbf{C_1}$ is done; if its value is **false** then $\mathbf{C_2}$ is done (in any other case an error occurs).

(C4) **while E do C**

If the value of **E** is **true** then **C** is done and then **while E do C** is repeated starting with the state resulting from **C**'s execution. If the value of **E** is **false** then nothing is done. If the value of **E** is neither **true** nor **false** an error occurs.

(C5) $\mathbf{C_1;C_2}$

$\mathbf{C_1}$ and then $\mathbf{C_2}$ are done in that order.

2.3. An example

The following TINY command outputs the sum of the numbers on the input. The end of the input is marked with **true**.

sum: = 0; x: = read;
while not (x = true) do (sum: = sum + x; x: = read);
output sum

2.4. Formal semantics of TINY

We shall now begin to formalize the above description of TINY. Our hope is to convey the general 'shape' of a denotational description. The reader should not attempt to grasp all the details (some of which are over-simplified) but just to get the main ideas.

An essential part of our formalization will be the definition of various sets (for example sets of denotations). It turns out that some of the ways of defining sets we need only work properly if we use certain special sets called *domains.* We shall thus use "domain" instead of "set"—however, intuitively, domains can be thought of just like sets (indeed the class of domains is just a subclass of the class of sets) and we shall employ normal set theoretic notation on them. For example $\{\mathbf{x} \mid P[\mathbf{x}]\}$ is the set of all **x**'s satisfying $P[\mathbf{x}]$; $\mathbf{x} \varepsilon \mathbf{S}$ means **x** belongs to **S**; $\mathbf{f}:\mathbf{S}_1 \rightarrow \mathbf{S}_2$ means **f** is a function from $\mathbf{S}_1$ to $\mathbf{S}_2$. In the next chapter (in fact in 3.2.) we shall explain why domains rather than sets must be used.

2.4.1. Syntax

To deal with the syntax we define the following *syntactic domains*:

$$\begin{aligned}\mathbf{Ide} &= \{\mathbf{I} \mid \mathbf{I} \text{ is an identifier}\}\\ \mathbf{Exp} &= \{\mathbf{E} \mid \mathbf{E} \text{ is an expression}\}\\ \mathbf{Com} &= \{\mathbf{C} \mid \mathbf{C} \text{ is a command}\}\end{aligned}$$

Domain names like these will always start with a capital letter. **Ide** is a standard domain; **Exp** and **Com** vary from language to language.

2.4.2. States, memories, inputs, outputs and values

We start by formalizing the concept of a state. To do this we define domains **State** of states, **Memory** of memories, **Input** of inputs, **Output** of outputs and **Value** of values. The definition of these domains consists of the following *domain equations* which we first state and then explain:

$$\begin{aligned}&\text{(i)} & \mathbf{State} &= \mathbf{Memory} \times \mathbf{Input} \times \mathbf{Output}\\ &\text{(ii)} & \mathbf{Memory} &= \mathbf{Ide} \rightarrow [\mathbf{Value} + \{\mathbf{unbound}\}]\\ &\text{(iii)} & \mathbf{Input} &= \mathbf{Value}^*\\ &\text{(iv)} & \mathbf{Output} &= \mathbf{Value}^*\\ &\text{(v)} & \mathbf{Value} &= \mathbf{Num} + \mathbf{Bool}\end{aligned}$$

(i) Means that **State** is the domain of all triples **(m,i,o)** where $\mathbf{m} \varepsilon \mathbf{Memory}$, $\mathbf{i} \varepsilon \mathbf{Input}$ and $\mathbf{o} \varepsilon \mathbf{Output}$. In general $\mathbf{D}_1 \times \mathbf{D}_2 \times \ldots \times \mathbf{D}_n$ is the domain $\{(\mathbf{d}_1,\mathbf{d}_2,\ldots,\mathbf{d}_n) \mid \mathbf{d}_1 \varepsilon \mathbf{D}_1, \mathbf{d}_2 \varepsilon \mathbf{D}_2, \ldots, \mathbf{d}_n \varepsilon \mathbf{D}_n\}$ of n-tuples.

(ii) Means that **Memory** is the domain of all functions from the domain **Ide** to the domain $[\mathbf{Value} + \{\mathbf{unbound}\}]$. The domain $[\mathbf{Value} + \{\mathbf{unbound}\}]$ is the union of the domain **Value** and the one-element domain $\{\mathbf{unbound}\}$. In general $[\mathbf{D}_1 \rightarrow \mathbf{D}_2]$ is the domain $\{\mathbf{f} \mid \mathbf{f}:\mathbf{D}_1 \rightarrow \mathbf{D}_2\}$ of all functions from $\mathbf{D}_1$ to $\mathbf{D}_2$ and $[\mathbf{D}_1 + \mathbf{D}_2]$ is the 'disjoint union' of $\mathbf{D}_1$ and $\mathbf{D}_2$—we clarify this later; for now, think of + as ordinary union restricted to disjoint domains. If $\mathbf{m} \varepsilon \mathbf{Memory}$ and $\mathbf{I} \varepsilon \mathbf{Ide}$ then **m I**, the result of applying the function **m** to argument **I**, is either in **Value** or is **unbound**; in the former case the value **m I** is the value bound to **I** in **m**; in the latter case **I** is unbound in **m**.

(iii) Means **Input** is the domain of all strings (including the empty string) of members of **Value**. In general **D*** is the domain

$$\{(\mathbf{d}_1,\ldots,\mathbf{d}_n) \mid \mathbf{d}_1 \varepsilon \mathbf{D}, \mathbf{d}_2 \varepsilon \mathbf{D}, \ldots, \mathbf{d}_n \varepsilon \mathbf{D}\}$$

of strings or sequences over **D**. We shall denote the empty string by **( )** and sometimes write $\mathbf{d}_1 . \mathbf{d}_2 . \ldots . \mathbf{d}_n$ instead of $(\mathbf{d}_1,\ldots,\mathbf{d}_n)$.

(iv) Means **Output** is the domain of all strings of values.

(v) Means that a value is either a number (i.e. a member of **Num**) or a truth value (i.e. a member of **Bool**). **Num** = {**0,1,2,...**} and **Bool** = {**true, false**}. Thus a state is a triple **(m,i,o)** where **m** is a function from identifiers to values (or **unbound**) and **i** and **o** are sequences of values.

2.4.3. Semantic functions

In this section we discuss the *semantic functions* for TINY. Semantic functions are functions which define the denotation of constructs. For TINY we need:

E:**Exp**→{denotations of expressions}
C:**Com**→{denotations of commands}

If **E**ε**Exp** and **C**ε**Com** then **E**[**E**] and **C**[**C**] are the results of applying the functions **E** and **C** to **E** and **C** respectively, and are the denotation of the corresponding constructs defined by the semantics. We discuss these denotations later, but first note that:

(i) In general if **X** is a variable which ranges over some syntactic domain of constructs then we will use **X** for the corresponding semantic functions. Thus **C**[**I: = E**] is the denotation—or meaning—of **I: = E** etc.

(ii) The "emphatic brackets" **[** and **]** are used to surround syntactic objects when applying semantic functions to them. They are supposed to increase readability but have no other significance—**X**[**X**] is just the result of applying the function **X** to **X**.

2.4.3.1. Denotations of expressions

Since expressions produce values one might at first take their denotations to be members of **Value**. To model this idea one would give the semantic function **E** the type **Exp**→**Value** and then **E**[**E**] would be **E**'s value (e.g. **E**[**0**] = **0**). This works for constant expressions but in general it fails to handle:

(i) The possibility of expressions causing errors (for example **1** + **true**).

(ii) The dependence of some expression's values on the state (for example the value of **x + 1** depends on what **x** is bound to in the memory; the value of **read** depends on the input).

(iii) The possibility that the evaluation of an expression might change the state (for example **read** removes the first item from the input).

To handle (i) we must define $\mathbf{E}$:**Exp**→[**Value** + {**error**}] so that:

$$\mathbf{E}[\mathbf{E}] = \begin{cases} \mathbf{v} & \text{if } \mathbf{v} \text{ is } \mathbf{E}\text{'s value} \\ \mathbf{error} & \text{if } \mathbf{E} \text{ causes an error} \end{cases}$$

For example, $\mathbf{E}[\mathbf{1} + \mathbf{1}] = \mathbf{2}$ but $\mathbf{E}[\mathbf{1} + \mathbf{true}] = \mathbf{error}$.

To handle (ii) we must make the result of an evaluation a function of the state—i.e. define $\mathbf{E}$:**Exp**→[**State**→[**Value** + {**error**}]] so that:

$$\mathbf{E}[\mathbf{E}]\mathbf{s} = \begin{cases} \mathbf{v} & \text{if } \mathbf{v} \text{ is } \mathbf{E}\text{'s value in } \mathbf{s} \\ \mathbf{error} & \text{if the evaluation causes an error} \end{cases}$$

For example:

$$\mathbf{E}[\mathbf{1} + \mathbf{x}]\mathbf{s} = \begin{cases} \mathbf{1} + (\mathbf{mx}) & \text{if } \mathbf{s} = (\mathbf{m}, \mathbf{i}, \mathbf{o}) \text{ and } \mathbf{mx} \text{ is a number} \\ \mathbf{error} & \text{otherwise} \end{cases}$$

Thus the denotation $\mathbf{E}[\mathbf{E}]$ of $\mathbf{E}$ is a function of type

$$\mathbf{Exp} \rightarrow [\mathbf{State} \rightarrow [\mathbf{Value} + \{\mathbf{error}\}]].$$

Finally to handle (iii) we must further complicate **E**'s type so that:

$$\mathbf{E}: \mathbf{Exp} \rightarrow [\mathbf{State} \rightarrow [[\mathbf{Value} \times \mathbf{State}] + \{\mathbf{error}\}]]$$

and then

$$\mathbf{E}[\mathbf{E}]\mathbf{s} = \begin{cases} (\mathbf{v}, \mathbf{s}') & \text{where } \mathbf{v} \text{ is } \mathbf{E}\text{'s value in } \mathbf{s} \text{ and } \mathbf{s}' \text{ is the state after the evaluation.} \\ \mathbf{error} & \text{if an error occurs.} \end{cases}$$

For example:

$$\mathbf{E[read]s} = \begin{cases} \mathbf{(hd\ i, (m, tl\ i, o))} & \text{if } \mathbf{s = (m, i, o)}, \mathbf{i} \text{ is non empty and has first member } \mathbf{hd\ i} \text{ and the rest is } \mathbf{tl\ i}. \\ \mathbf{error} & \text{if the input is empty.} \end{cases}$$

We formally define **E** by cases on the different kinds of expressions. For example, the denotations of expressions of the form **I** are defined by the following *semantic clause*:

$$\mathbf{E[I]\,(m, i, o)} = \mathbf{(m\,I = unbound) \rightarrow error, (mI, (m, i, o))}$$

Here "$\mathbf{b} \rightarrow \mathbf{v}_1, \mathbf{v}_2$" means "if **b** is true then $\mathbf{v}_1$ else $\mathbf{v}_2$"—we give a precise account of this notation in 3.4.5. Thus the above semantic clause says that if **m I** is **unbound** (i.e. **I** is unbound in **m**) then an error occurs; otherwise the value of **I** is whatever it is bound to in the memory. The state resulting from the evaluation is **(m, i, o)**—i.e. the original state. An example of a semantic clause in which the evaluation changes the state is:

$$\mathbf{E[read]\,(m, i, o) = null\ i \rightarrow error, (hd\ i, (m, tl\ i, o))}$$

Here **null i** is true if **i** is empty, **hd i** is the first element of **i** and **tl i** the rest (see 3.3.3.3.). Thus, if the input is empty, an error results; otherwise the value of **read** is the first item in the input and the resulting state has this item removed.

The rest of the semantic clauses for TINY are described in 2.4.4. below.

2.4.3.2. Denotations of commands

The effect of executing a command is to produce a new state or generate an error; thus:

$$\mathbf{C:Com \rightarrow [State \rightarrow [State + \{error\}]]}$$

a typical semantic clause is:

$$\mathbf{C[output\ E]\,s} = \mathbf{(E[E]s = (v, (m, i, o))) \rightarrow (m, i, v\,.\,o), error}$$

Here **v. o** is the string resulting from sticking **v** onto the front of **o**. Thus this semantic clause says that **C[output E]** is a function which when applied to a state **s** first evaluates **E**, and if **E** produces a value **v** and new state **(m, i, o),** then the result is **(m, i, v. o);** otherwise the result is **error.**

2.4.4. Semantic clauses

In this section we describe and explain the semantic clauses for TINY.

2.4.4.1. Clauses for expressions

(E1) **E[0]s = (0, s)**
E[1]s = (1, s)

The value of a numeral is the corresponding number; the evaluation does not change the state.

(E2) **E[true]s = (true, s)**
E[false]s = (false, s)

The value of a boolean constant is the corresponding boolean value (truth value); the evaluation does not change the state.

(E3) **E[read] (m, i, o) = null i→error, (hd i, (m, tl i, o))**

This was explained above, **null i** is **true** if **i** is empty, and **false** otherwise; **hd i** is the first element of **i** and **tl i** is the rest of **i**.

(E4) **E[I] (m, i, o) = (m I = unbound)→error, (m I, (m, i, o))**

This was explained in 2.4.3.1. above.

(E5) **E[not E] s = (E[E]s = (v,s′))→(isBool v→(not v,s′), error), error**

isBool v is **true** if **v**ε**Bool** and is **false** otherwise (here **v**ε**Value = Num + Bool**); **not: Bool→Bool** is the function defined by **not true = false** and **not false = true**. Thus the value of **not E** is **not** of the value of **E** (or **error** if **E**'s evaluation leads to a number or **error**) and the state is changed to the state **s**′ resulting from **E**'s evaluation in **s**.

(E6) $\mathbf{E[E_1 = E_2]\, s = (E[E_1]s = (v_1, s_1)) \to ((E[E_2]s_1 = (v_2, s_2)) \to}$
$\mathbf{(v_1 = v_2, s_2), error), error}$

Here $\mathbf{v_1 = v_2}$ is **true** if $\mathbf{v_1}$ equals $\mathbf{v_2}$ and **false** otherwise. Thus the result of $\mathbf{E_1 = E_2}$ in **s** is obtained by first evaluating $\mathbf{E_1}$ in **s** to get $\mathbf{(v_1, s_1)}$ (or **error** —in which case **error** is the value of $\mathbf{E_1 = E_2}$), then evaluating $\mathbf{E_2}$ in $\mathbf{s_1}$ to get $(\mathbf{v_2}, \mathbf{s_2})$ (or **error**—in which case **error** is the value of $\mathbf{E_1} = \mathbf{E_2}$), and finally returning $(\mathbf{v_1} = \mathbf{v_2}, \mathbf{s_2})$ as the result of $\mathbf{E_1} = \mathbf{E_2}$.

(E7) $$\mathbf{E}[\![\mathbf{E_1} + \mathbf{E_2}]\!]\mathbf{s} = (\mathbf{E}[\![\mathbf{E_1}]\!]\mathbf{s} = (\mathbf{v_1}, \mathbf{s_1})) \rightarrow ((\mathbf{E}[\![\mathbf{E_2}]\!]\mathbf{s_1} = (\mathbf{v_2}, \mathbf{s_2})) \rightarrow (\mathbf{isNum}\ \mathbf{v_1}\ \mathbf{and}\ \mathbf{isNum}\ \mathbf{v_2} \rightarrow (\mathbf{v_1} + \mathbf{v_2}, \mathbf{s_2}), \mathbf{error}), \mathbf{error}), \mathbf{error}$$

This semantic clause is similar to the preceding one. **isNum v** is **true** if **v** is a number (i.e. member of **Num**) and **false** otherwise. Thus (E7) says that to evaluate $\mathbf{E_1} + \mathbf{E_2}$ one evaluates $\mathbf{E_1}$, then evaluates $\mathbf{E_2}$ (in the state resulting from $\mathbf{E_1}$), then tests their values to make sure they are numbers, and if so returns their sum and the state resulting from $\mathbf{E_2}$. If either of these values is not a number or if $\mathbf{E_1}$ or $\mathbf{E_2}$ generates an error then $\mathbf{E_1} + \mathbf{E_2}$ generates an error.

2.4.4.2. Clauses for commands

(C1) $$\mathbf{C}[\![\mathbf{I} := \mathbf{E}]\!]\,\mathbf{s} = (\mathbf{E}[\![\mathbf{E}]\!]\mathbf{s} = (\mathbf{v}, (\mathbf{m}, \mathbf{i}, \mathbf{o}))) \rightarrow (\mathbf{m}[\mathbf{v}/\mathbf{I}], \mathbf{i}, \mathbf{o}), \mathbf{error}$$

$$(\mathbf{m}[\mathbf{v}/\mathbf{I}])\,\mathbf{I}' = \begin{cases} \mathbf{v} & \text{if } \mathbf{I} = \mathbf{I}' \\ \mathbf{m}\,\mathbf{I}' & \text{otherwise} \end{cases}$$

Thus $\mathbf{C}[\![\mathbf{I} := \mathbf{E}]\!]\,\mathbf{s}$ is a state identical to the state resulting from the evaluation of **E**, except that **E**'s value **v** is bound to **I** in the memory (if **E** produces **error** then so does **I**: = **E**).

(C2) $$\mathbf{C}[\![\mathbf{output}\ \mathbf{E}]\!]\,\mathbf{s} = (\mathbf{E}[\![\mathbf{E}]\!]\mathbf{s} = (\mathbf{v}, (\mathbf{m}, \mathbf{i}, \mathbf{o}))) \rightarrow (\mathbf{m}, \mathbf{i}, \mathbf{v} . \mathbf{o}), \mathbf{error}$$

The semantic clause was explained in 2.4.3.2. above.

(C3) $$\mathbf{C}[\![\mathbf{if}\ \mathbf{E}\ \mathbf{then}\ \mathbf{C_1}\ \mathbf{else}\ \mathbf{C_2}]\!]\,\mathbf{s} = (\mathbf{E}[\![\mathbf{E}]\!]\,\mathbf{s} = (\mathbf{v}, \mathbf{s}')) \rightarrow (\mathbf{isBool}\ \mathbf{v} \rightarrow (\mathbf{v} \rightarrow \mathbf{C}[\![\mathbf{C_1}]\!]\,\mathbf{s}', \mathbf{C}[\![\mathbf{C_2}]\!]\,\mathbf{s}'), \mathbf{error}), \mathbf{error}$$

isBool v is **true** if **v** is a truth value (i.e. if $\mathbf{v} \varepsilon \mathbf{Bool} = \{\mathbf{true}, \mathbf{false}\}$) and is **false** otherwise. Thus if **E** produces result $(\mathbf{v}, \mathbf{s}')$ when evaluated in **s** then $\mathbf{C_1}$ or $\mathbf{C_2}$ is executed (in the state $\mathbf{s}'$ resulting from **E**) depending on whether **E**'s value **v** is **true** or **false**.

(C4) $\mathbf{C}$**[while E do C] s =**
($\mathbf{E}$[E] s = (v,s′))→
(isBool v→
(v→(($\mathbf{C}$[C] s′ = s″)→$\mathbf{C}$[while E do C] s″,error),s′),
error),error

If **E** produces an error then so does **while E do C**; if **E** produces value **v** and a new state **s′**, then if **v** is **true, C** is done to get **s″** and then **while E do C** is done starting with **s″**. If **v** is **false,** then the result of **while E do C** is **s′**, the result of **E**. Finally, if **v** is not a truth value or $\mathbf{C}$[**C**]**s′** = **error,** then **while E do C** causes an error. Notice that (C4) is *recursive* because $\mathbf{C}$[**while E do s**] occurs on the right hand side.

(C5) $\mathbf{C}[\mathbf{C}_1;\mathbf{C}_2]\,\mathbf{s} = (\mathbf{C}[\mathbf{C}_1]\mathbf{s}=\mathbf{error})\rightarrow\mathbf{error},\mathbf{C}[\mathbf{C}_2](\mathbf{C}[\mathbf{C}_1]\mathbf{s})$

Thus if $\mathbf{C}_1$ generates an error then so does $\mathbf{C}_1;\mathbf{C}_2$; otherwise $\mathbf{C}_2$ is done in the state resulting from $\mathbf{C}_1$.

This completes the semantic clauses, and also the formal semantics, of TINY. In some of the clauses, especially (E6), (E7), (C3) and (C4), the tests for the various error conditions make it hard to follow what is going on—the semantics of non-error executions fail to stand out. In the next chapter we describe various notations for clarifying and simplifying semantic clauses; the reader may like to peep ahead to chapter 4 to see how neat the clauses can be made.

An important thing to note about the semantic clauses above is that each construct has its denotation defined in terms of the denotation of its components; for example $\mathbf{C}[\mathbf{C}_1;\ \mathbf{C}_2]$ is defined in terms of $\mathbf{C}[\mathbf{C}_1]$ and $\mathbf{C}[\mathbf{C}_2]$. The only exception to this is (C4), the clause for **while E do C**, where the denotation is defined 'in terms of itself'—we shall have more to say on such recursive definitions in 3.2.1.

2.4.5. Summary of the formal semantics of TINY

The formal semantic description of TINY just given had three main parts:

(i) Specification of the syntactic domains **Exp** and **Com**.
(ii) Specification of the semantic domains **State, Value,** etc.
(iii) Specification of the semantic functions $\mathbf{E}$ and $\mathbf{C}$ which map syntactic entities to semantic ones.

In the next chapter we shall describe in detail the concepts and notations of these specifications. In subsequent chapters we shall refine and extend the concepts and notation, and apply the techniques to a wide variety of programming constructs (including most of ALGOL 60 and PASCAL).

3. General concepts and notation

This chapter is rather long and tedious—it is a 'user manual' for the notation and concepts we shall need. On first reading one should only look in detail at 3.1. and 3.2.; the other sections should be quickly skimmed and then referred to later when their contents are used. Here is a quick overview of the main sections:

3.1. We explain the concept of 'abstract syntax'—the kind of syntactic description convenient for semantics.
3.2. We explain why we use "domains" rather than sets and discuss informally the role of the underlying mathematical theories.
3.3. We describe different kinds of domains and ways of building them.
3.4. We discuss the concept of a function and then describe numerous notations for manipulating functions.

3.1. Abstract syntax

The programs of most languages are built out of various kinds of *constructs* such as identifiers, expressions, commands and declarations. For example, let **C** be the TINY command **x: = read; sum: = sum + x**; then:

C is the command $\mathbf{C}_1;\mathbf{C}_2$
  where $\mathbf{C}_1$ is the command $\mathbf{I}_1 := \mathbf{E}_1$
    where $\mathbf{I}_1$ is the identifier **x**
    and $\mathbf{E}_1$ is the expression **read**
  and $\mathbf{C}_2$ is the command $\mathbf{I}_2 := \mathbf{E}_2$
    where $\mathbf{I}_2$ is the identifier **sum**
    and $\mathbf{E}_2$ is the expression $\mathbf{E}_{21} + \mathbf{E}_{22}$
      where $\mathbf{E}_{21}$ is the identifier **sum**
      and $\mathbf{E}_{22}$ is the identifier **x**

We call the various constructs which make up a given construct its *constituents;* for example, $\mathbf{C}_1$, $\mathbf{C}_2$, $\mathbf{I}_1$, $\mathbf{I}_2$, $\mathbf{E}_1$, $\mathbf{E}_2$, $\mathbf{E}_{21}$, $\mathbf{E}_{22}$ are the constituents of **C**. The *immediate constituents* of a construct are its 'biggest' constituents; for example, the immediate constituents of **C** are $\mathbf{C}_1$ and $\mathbf{C}_2$, the immediate constituents of $\mathbf{C}_1$ are $\mathbf{I}_1$ and $\mathbf{E}_1$ and the immediate constituents of $\mathbf{C}_2$ are $\mathbf{I}_2$ and $\mathbf{E}_2$.

As we noted after listing the semantic clauses of TINY, the denotation assigned to a construct by a denotational semantics depends only on the kind of construct and the denotations of its immediate constituent. Thus for the purposes of semantics a syntactic description need only specify the various constructs and what their immediate constituents are. Other details of syntax—for example precedence—are irrelevant for semantics and can thus be ignored. A syntactic description which just lists the kinds of constructs and their immediate constituents is called an *abstract syntax*.

The notation we shall use to specify abstract syntax has two parts:

(i) A list of the various *syntactic categories* of the language (for TINY the syntactic categories are expressions and commands). For each category we provide a name for the domain of all constructs of that category (for TINY the names are "**Exp**" and "**Com**") and a *metavariable* to range over the domain (in TINY, **E** ranges over **Exp** and **C** ranges over **Com**).

(ii) A list of *syntactic clauses*, each one specifying the various kinds of constructs in a category (for TINY, the syntactic clauses were given in 2.1., namely **E :: = 0** | ..., and **C :: = I: = E** | ...).

The metavariables stand for constructs of the corresponding category (i.e. members of the corresponding syntactic domain). To distinguish different instances metavariables may be primed or subscripted (for example, $\mathbf{E}$, $\mathbf{E}'$, $\mathbf{E}_1$, $\mathbf{E}_2$, stand for expressions). The notation for each kind of construct given in the syntactic clauses must display the immediate constituents and distinguish it from other kinds of construct, but otherwise it is arbitrary. Usually one chooses a notation based on some actual concrete syntax for the language being defined.

We shall always use a fixed standard domain **Ide** of *identifiers* (with metavariable **I**). Although languages do in fact differ in what they allow as identifiers these differences are not normally *semantically* significant.

3.2. Sets and domains

In describing the semantics of TINY we mysteriously used the word "domain" instead of "set". As we hinted, this was for technical mathematical reasons. Unfortunately to fully explain the difference between sets and domains, and to convincingly justify our use of the latter, we would have to delve in detail into the underlying mathematics. This we wish to avoid, and so I shall just very crudely sketch some of the issues involved. Readers who are not satisfied with this discussion should consult Joe Stoy's excellent book [Stoy] where all details are lucidly explained.

There are really two related, but separate, problems which lead to the use of domains rather than sets:

(i) Recursive definitions of functions.
(ii) Recursive definitions of sets.

We shall look at these in turn.

3.2.1. The problem of recursively defined functions

We often find it necessary to define functions recursively. For example, the semantic clause for **while E do C**, (C4), defines **C[while E do C]** as some expression involving **C[while E do C]**. At first sight such 'definitions' are highly suspicious since they seem to assume that the thing they are trying to define is already defined. The way out is to regard recursive definitions as *equations*—to regard (C4) as analogous to the quadratic equation $\mathbf{x}=\frac{1}{3}\mathbf{x}^2+\frac{2}{3}$ (which 'defines' **x** to be **1** or **2**) and to seek methods of solving functional equations, like (C4), analogous to the methods we have for solving quadratic equations. It turns out that the kind of functional equations we want to solve in semantics only have solutions when the functions involved map between specially structured sets called domains. To see what goes wrong with ordinary sets consider the following two equations 'defining' **f: Num→Num**

(i) **f x = (f x) + 1**
(ii) **f x = f x**

If **Num** = {**0,1,2,...**} there is *no* **f** satisfying (i) and *every* **f** satisfies (ii); thus neither of these two equations in any sense defines **f**. On the other hand the equation

(iii) **f x = (x = 0)→1,x × f(x-1)**

uniquely defines **f** to be the factorial function (i.e. for all **x:f x = x!**). If we used arbitrary sets then it would be just as easy to write bad definitions like (i) and (ii) as good ones like (iii). What the theory of domains does is ensure that *every* definition is good. It does this by:

(a) Requiring all domains to have a certain 'implicit structure' which can be shown to guarantee that all equations (including (i), (ii) and (iii)) have at least one solution.

(b) Providing a way, via the 'implicit structure', of choosing an 'intended solution' from among the various solutions guaranteed by (a).

For example, the domain **Num**, in virtue of its 'implicit structure', contains, besides **0**, **1**, **2**, ..., an 'undefined' element **undefined;** then (i) and (ii) both end up defining **f** to be the 'undefined function': **f x = undefined** for all **x**ε**Num**. (iii) defines **f** to satisfy **f x = x!** if **x = 0**, **x = 1**, ... and **f undefined = undefined**. We shall not go into the details obscurely hinted at here; all the reader needs to know is that recursive definitions can be solved in a way that justifies the intuitions behind them. Some further discussion on recursive definitions occurs in 3.4.9.

3.2.2. The problem of recursively defined sets

It is often the case that intuitions about the 'data' manipulated by programs in a language lead us to want to define *recursively* the domains modelling the corresponding 'data-types'. As an example let us examine one way of adding parameterless procedures to TINY. We add to the syntax of TINY a new kind of expression **proc C** and a new kind of command **I**. The informal semantics of these is:

(E8) **proc C**

The value of **proc C** is a procedure which when invoked (by an identifier denoting it) executes **C**.

(C6) **I**

When the command **I** is executed the procedure denoted by **I** is invoked.

For example in a program

```
P := proc (x := x+1);
              :
P;
              :
P;
              :
```

each time a **P** was executed, **x** would be incremented by **1**.

To handle the formal semantics we must extend the domain **Value** to include the denotations of procedures. Thus:

$$\mathbf{Value} = \mathbf{Num} + \mathbf{Bool} + \mathbf{Proc}$$

For denotations of procedures we simply take the state transformation done each time the procedure is invoked. Thus

$$\mathbf{Proc} = \mathbf{State} \rightarrow [\mathbf{State} + \{\mathbf{error}\}]$$

Now the semantic clauses are simply:

(E8) $\mathcal{E}[\![\mathbf{proc\ C}]\!]\,\mathbf{s} = (\mathcal{C}[\![\mathbf{C}]\!],\mathbf{s})$

(C6) $\mathcal{C}[\![\mathbf{I}]\!](\mathbf{m},\mathbf{i},\mathbf{o}) = \mathbf{isProc}(\mathbf{m\ I}) \rightarrow \mathbf{m\ I}\,(\mathbf{m},\mathbf{i},\mathbf{o})\ ,\ \mathbf{error}$

Here **m I (m,i,o)** is the procedure value **m I** denoted by **I** in **m** applied to the state **(m,i,o)**. To see the point of this example let us write out the domain equations for this extended TINY:

$$\begin{aligned}
\mathbf{State} &= \mathbf{Memory} \times \mathbf{Input} \times \mathbf{Output}\\
\mathbf{Memory} &= \mathbf{Ide} \rightarrow [\mathbf{Value} + \{\mathbf{unbound}\}]\\
\mathbf{Input} &= \mathbf{Value}^*\\
\mathbf{Output} &= \mathbf{Value}^*\\
\mathbf{Value} &= \mathbf{Num} + \mathbf{Bool} + \mathbf{Proc}\\
\mathbf{Proc} &= \mathbf{State} \rightarrow [\mathbf{State} + \{\mathbf{error}\}]
\end{aligned}$$

These domain equations are recursive: **State** is defined in terms of **Memory,** which is defined in terms of **Value,** which is defined in terms of **Proc,** which is defined in terms of **State**. Thus just as the 'looping' of **while E do C** led us to define its denotation as a recursive *function*, so the embedding of procedures in states leads us to define **State** as a recursive *domain.* Now just as there are problems with recursive definitions of functions, so there are problems—much harder problems, in fact—with recursive definitions of domains. For example, it can be shown mathematically that there are no *sets* satisfying the domain equations above! Fortunately if we work with domains, and interpret the domain building operators $\times$, $\rightarrow$, $+$ in a clever way, then solutions do exist. In other words set equations cannot in general be solved, but domain equations can. The crucial two ideas which ensure all domain equations have solutions are firstly to define $[\mathbf{D}_1 \rightarrow \mathbf{D}_2]$ to be the domain, not of all functions, but just of those functions which preserve the 'implicit structure' on the domains $\mathbf{D}_1$ and $\mathbf{D}_2$ (this 'implicit structure' is present as a consequence of the exact definition of a domain), and secondly to interpret $=$ not as equality between domains but as 'isomorphism'. Alas, we cannot explain these tantalising remarks further here.

3.2.3. The role of Dana Scott's theory

A major breakthrough in semantic theory came when Dana Scott showed [Scott] how to consistently interpret both kinds of recursive definitions—definitions of members of domains (see 3.2.1.) and definitions of domains themselves (see 3.2.2.)—in a single unified framework. In summary what he did was:

(i) Devise a class of 'structured' sets called domains and define the operators $\times$, $+$, $\rightarrow$, $*$ etc. on them.
(ii) Show how elements of domains could be defined recursively.
(iii) Show how domains themselves could be defined recursively.

Many of the intuitive ideas of denotational semantics have been around for ages—for example, in 1966 Strachey published a paper "Towards a Formal Semantics" [Strachey] which contains several of the key concepts described in this book, and even before that John McCarthy had outlined what was essentially a denotational semantics of a fragment of ALGOL 60 [McCarthy].

The main achievement of Dana Scott was firstly to point out that the naive formalization of some of the early semantic models could not be consistently extended to non-trivial languages, and then to show how a consistent (and very beautiful) theory was in fact possible if domains (instead of arbitrary sets) were used to model denotations.

The problem with inconsistent formalizations (like Strachey's potentially was) is that they provide no basis for reliable reasoning. For example, consider the proof of **1** = **2** that proceeds by first assuming **0** = **1** and then adding **1** to both sides—proofs of properties of programs from inconsistent formalizations are just like this!

Of course the early inconsistent theories were not without value; for one thing they prompted the discovery of the modern consistent versions. It is usually easier to formalize ideas than to think of them and the early pioneers of semantics must take the credit for originating the general approach, if not the fine details. There are plenty of other examples of inconsistent ideas being useful—for example the use of infinitesimals in calculus and the use of Dirac delta-functions in physics; both these were valuable for years (indeed centuries) before consistent models of them were devised.

Thus, although the idea of denotational semantics is quite old, it was nevertheless a major breakthrough when in 1969 Scott formulated his theory; for only then could we start to use semantic models as the basis for *trustworthy* proofs. Furthermore his theory has enormously sharpened our intuitions about the concepts involved and it is inconceivable that the descriptive techniques described in this book could have advanced as fast as they have without it. Also it seems that future developments in semantics (for example, to handle concurrency [Milne and Milner]) will be even more dependent on the underlying theory.

3.2.4. The role of mathematics in the book

We shall not discuss the mathematics involved in Scott's theory at all; our approach to recursive equations is similar to an engineer's approach to differential equations; we assume they have solutions but don't bother with the mathematical justification. In practice this is perfectly satisfactory for the kinds of things we discuss in this book; one only needs to dabble in the mathematics if:

(i) One wishes to perform rigorous proofs.
(ii) One wishes to devise descriptive techniques for radically different kinds of constructs (for example involving concurrency).

3.3. Defining domains

In this section we explain all the ways we shall need of defining domains. $\mathbf{D}$, $\mathbf{D}'$, $\mathbf{D}_1$, $\mathbf{D}_2$, ... etc. will stand for arbitrary domains and the name of any particular domain will start with a capital letter (for example: **Num**, **Value**, **State**).

3.3.1. Standard domains

The following domains are standard and will be used without further explanation:

numbers: **Num** $=\{\mathbf{0, 1, 2, \ldots}\}$
truth values: **Bool** $=\{\mathbf{true, false}\}$
identifiers: **Ide** $=\{\mathbf{I} \mid \mathbf{I}$ is a string of letters or digits beginning with a letter$\}$

3.3.2. Finite domains

Finite domains will be defined explicitly by listing their elements; for example:

Spectrum $=\{$**red, orange, yellow, green, blue, indigo, violet**$\}$

3.3.3. Domain constructors

We shall build domains out of standard, or finite, domains using the various *domain constructors* described below. Since we are avoiding the underlying mathematics some of the descriptions will be slightly oversimplified; these oversimplifications only concern technical details and do not affect the main ideas.

3.3.3.1. Function space $[\mathbf{D}_1 \to \mathbf{D}_2]$

$[\mathbf{D}_1 \to \mathbf{D}_2]$ is the domain of functions from $\mathbf{D}_1$ to $\mathbf{D}_2$.

$$[\mathbf{D}_1 \to \mathbf{D}_2] = \{\mathbf{f} \mid \mathbf{f}: \mathbf{D}_1 \to \mathbf{D}_2\}$$

Comments (i) $\mathbf{f} \varepsilon [\mathbf{D}_1 \to \mathbf{D}_2]$ if and only if $\mathbf{f}: \mathbf{D}_1 \to \mathbf{D}_2$ and we say "**f** has type $\mathbf{D}_1 \to \mathbf{D}_2$". In general for any domain **D** (not necessarily a function space), if $\mathbf{d} \varepsilon \mathbf{D}$ we say "**d** has type **D**" and write "**d: D**".

(ii) If $\mathbf{f}\varepsilon[\mathbf{D}_1\rightarrow\mathbf{D}_2]$ then $\mathbf{D}_1$ is called the *source* of **f** and $\mathbf{D}_2$ the *target* of **f** (sometimes "domain" and "range" are used instead of "source" and "target"—but this conflicts with our other uses of the word "domain").

(iii) We may write $\mathbf{D}_1\rightarrow\mathbf{D}_2$ instead of $[\mathbf{D}_1\rightarrow\mathbf{D}_2]$; by convention→associates to the right, so for example,

$$\mathbf{D}_1\rightarrow\mathbf{D}_2\rightarrow\mathbf{D}_3\rightarrow\mathbf{D}_4 \text{ means } [\mathbf{D}_1\rightarrow[\mathbf{D}_2\rightarrow[\mathbf{D}_3\rightarrow\mathbf{D}_4]]].$$

(iv) In Scott's theory, $[\mathbf{D}_1\rightarrow\mathbf{D}_2]$ is defined to be the set of all functions which 'preserve the structure' of the domains; thus, strictly speaking, not every function is in $[\mathbf{D}_1\rightarrow\mathbf{D}_2]$. In practice all the functions we shall use—indeed all the functions our notations allow us to define—do 'preserve structure' and no problems arise. Our assumption that all functions are in $[\mathbf{D}_1\rightarrow\mathbf{D}_2]$ is analogous to the engineer's assumption that all functions are differentiable.

3.3.3.2. Product $[\mathbf{D}_1\times\mathbf{D}_2\times\ldots\times\mathbf{D}_n]$

$[\mathbf{D}_1\times\mathbf{D}_2\times\ldots\times\mathbf{D}_n]$ is the domain of all n-tuples $(\mathbf{d}_1, \mathbf{d}_2, \ldots, \mathbf{d}_n)$ of elements $\mathbf{d}_1\varepsilon\mathbf{D}_1, \mathbf{d}_2\varepsilon\mathbf{D}_2, \ldots, \mathbf{d}_n\varepsilon\mathbf{D}_n$. If $\mathbf{d}\varepsilon[\mathbf{D}_1\times\mathbf{D}_2\times\ldots\times\mathbf{D}_n]$ then **el i d** is the **i**th coordinate of **d**. Thus

$$[\mathbf{D}_1\times\mathbf{D}_2\times\ldots\times\mathbf{D}_n]=\{(\mathbf{d}_1, \mathbf{d}_2, \ldots, \mathbf{d}_n) \mid \mathbf{d}_1\varepsilon\mathbf{D}_1, \mathbf{d}_2\varepsilon\mathbf{D}_2, \ldots, \mathbf{d}_n\varepsilon\mathbf{D}_n\}$$
$$\mathbf{el\ i}\ (\mathbf{d}_1, \mathbf{d}_2, \ldots, \mathbf{d}_n)=\mathbf{d}_i$$
$$\mathbf{d}=(\mathbf{el\ 1\ d}, \mathbf{el\ 2\ d}, \ldots, \mathbf{el\ n\ d})$$

3.3.3.3. Sequences D*

D* is the domain of all *finite* sequences of elements of **D**. If **dεD*** then either **d** is the empty sequence **( )** or $\mathbf{d}=(\mathbf{d}_1, \mathbf{d}_2, \ldots, \mathbf{d}_n)$ where **n>0** and each $\mathbf{d}_i$ is a member of **D**. As with the product, **el i d** is the **i**th coordinate of **d**; **hd d** is the first member of **d** (thus **hd d = el 1 d**) and **tl d** is the sequence consisting of all but the first element of **d**; **null d** is **true** if **d** is the empty string and **false** otherwise. Thus:

$$\mathbf{D^* = \{(d_1, d_2, \ldots, d_n) \mid 0 < n, d_i \varepsilon D\} + \{(\,)\}}$$

$$\mathbf{el\ i\ (d_1, d_2, \ldots, d_n) = d_i}$$
$$\mathbf{hd\ (d_1, d_2, \ldots, d_n) = d_1}$$
$$\mathbf{tl\ (d_1, d_2, \ldots, d_n) = (d_2, \ldots, d_n)}$$

$$\mathbf{null\ d} = \begin{cases} \mathbf{true} & \text{if } \mathbf{d = (\,)} \\ \mathbf{false} & \text{otherwise} \end{cases}$$

Comments (i) **el**, **hd**, **tl** and **null** can be thought of as functions with types:

$$\mathbf{el{:}Num \rightarrow D^* \rightarrow D}$$
$$\mathbf{hd{:}D^* \rightarrow D}$$
$$\mathbf{tl{:}D^* \rightarrow D^*}$$
$$\mathbf{null{:}D^* \rightarrow Bool}$$

el, **hd** and **tl** only make sense when applied to non-empty sequences.

(ii) An alternative notation for the sequence $\mathbf{(d_1, d_2, \ldots, d_n)}$ is $\mathbf{d_1 . d_2 . \ldots . d_n}$. Also if $\mathbf{d \varepsilon D}$ and $\mathbf{d^* = (d_1, d_2, \ldots, d_n) \varepsilon D^*}$ then $\mathbf{d . d^*}$ is the sequence $\mathbf{(d, d_1, d_2, \ldots, d_n)}$. When using this notation we may refer to sequences as *strings*.

3.3.3.4. Sum $\mathbf{[D_1 + D_2 + \ldots + D_n]}$

Each member of $\mathbf{[D_1 + D_2 + \ldots + D_n]}$ corresponds to *exactly one* member of some $\mathbf{D_i}$. The difference between the sum $\mathbf{[D_1 + D_2 + \ldots + D_n]}$ and the union of $\mathbf{D_1, \ldots, D_n}$ is that if **d** is in the union and $\mathbf{d \varepsilon D_i}$ and $\mathbf{d \varepsilon D_j}$ (for some $\mathbf{i \neq j}$), then it does not make sense to ask if **d** comes from $\mathbf{D_i}$ or $\mathbf{D_j}$. Each member of $\mathbf{[D_1 + D_2 + \ldots + D_n]}$ on the other hand is 'flagged' to indicate which domain it comes from. To make this clear we define

$$\mathbf{[D_1 + D_2 + \ldots + D_n] = \{(d_i, i) \mid d_i \varepsilon D_i, 0 < i < n+1\}}$$

so that if $\mathbf{d \varepsilon D_i}$ and $\mathbf{d \varepsilon D_j}$ then **(d, i)** represents **d** considered as a member of $\mathbf{D_i}$ and **(d, j)** represents **d** considered as a member of $\mathbf{D_j}$.

If $\mathbf{D = [D_1 + D_2 + \ldots + D_n]}$ and $\mathbf{d \varepsilon D}$ then $\mathbf{isD_i\ d}$ is **true** if **d** corresponds to a member of $\mathbf{D_i}$ and **false** otherwise. If $\mathbf{isD_i\ d = true}$ then $\mathbf{outD_i\ d}$ is the member of $\mathbf{D_i}$ corresponding to **d**. If $\mathbf{d_i \varepsilon D_i}$ then $\mathbf{inD_i d_i}$ is the member of **D** corresponding to $\mathbf{d_i}$. In summary:

$$[\mathbf{D_1 + D_2 + \ldots + D_n}] = \{(\mathbf{d_i}, \mathbf{i}) \mid \mathbf{d_i \varepsilon D_i}, 0 < \mathbf{i} < \mathbf{n} + 1\}$$

$$\mathbf{isD_i\ d} = \begin{cases} \mathbf{true} & \text{if } \mathbf{d} \text{ is of the form } (\mathbf{d_i}, \mathbf{i}). \\ \mathbf{false} & \text{otherwise.} \end{cases}$$

$$\mathbf{outD_i\ d} = \begin{cases} \mathbf{d_i} & \text{if } \mathbf{d} \text{ is of the form } (\mathbf{d_i}, \mathbf{i}) \\ \text{'undefined' otherwise} \end{cases}$$

$$\mathbf{inD_i\ d_i} = (\mathbf{d_i}, \mathbf{i})$$

Comments (i) $\mathbf{isD_i}$, $\mathbf{outD_i}$ and $\mathbf{inD_i}$ can be thought of as functions with types:

$$\mathbf{isD_i}:[\mathbf{D_1 + D_2 + \ldots + D_n}] \rightarrow \mathbf{Bool}$$
$$\mathbf{outD_i}:[\mathbf{D_1 + D_2 + \ldots + D_n}] \rightarrow \mathbf{D_i}$$
$$\mathbf{inD_i}:\mathbf{D_i} \rightarrow [\mathbf{D_1 + D_2 + \ldots + D_n}]$$

(ii) If two summands of a sum have the same name then this notation breaks down. For example, if **D = Num + Num + Bool** then **isNum d** is not well defined. We shall always have summands with distinct names—if one wants to avoid this restriction then a different notation must be used (for example **is1**, **is2**, **is3** etc., as tests for the first, second and third summands).

(iii) To avoid having to clutter up expressions with $\mathbf{inD_i}$ and $\mathbf{outD_i}$ we shall usually allow context to determine whether an element is in $\mathbf{D_i}$ or in **D** where $\mathbf{D} = [\mathbf{D_1 + D_2 + \ldots + D_n}]$. We thus adopt the following conventions which are analogous to the 'coercions' of programming languages.

(a) If $\mathbf{d_i \varepsilon D_i}$ occurs in a context requiring a member of $\mathbf{D} = [\mathbf{D_1 + D_2 + \ldots + D_n}]$ then we interpret the occurrence of $\mathbf{d_i}$ as $\mathbf{inD_i\ d_i}$. For example if $\mathbf{n \varepsilon Num}$, **Value = Num + Bool** and **f: Value→D** (some **D**) then "**f n**" really means "**f (inNum n)**".

(b) If $\mathbf{d}\varepsilon[\mathbf{D}_1 + \mathbf{D}_2 + \ldots + \mathbf{D}_n]$ occurs in a context requiring a member of $\mathbf{D}_i$ then we interpret the occurrence of **d** as $\mathbf{outD}_i\ \mathbf{d}$. For example, if **f: D→[Num + Bool]** and **g: Bool→D′** then "**g(f d)**" really means "**g(outBool (f d))**"

(iv) The domain **D*** of finite sequences can be thought of as an infinite sum

$$\mathbf{D}^* = \{(\,)\} + \mathbf{D} + [\mathbf{D} \times \mathbf{D}] + [\mathbf{D} \times \mathbf{D} \times \mathbf{D}] + \ldots$$

3.3.4. Domain equations

We discussed in 3.2.2. why we need to be able to define domains by recursive equations. In general such equations have the form

$$\begin{aligned} \mathbf{D}_1 &= T_1\,[\mathbf{D}_1, \ldots, \mathbf{D}_n] \\ \mathbf{D}_2 &= T_2\,[\mathbf{D}_1, \ldots, \mathbf{D}_n] \\ &\vdots \\ \mathbf{D}_n &= T_n\,[\mathbf{D}_1, \ldots, \mathbf{D}_n] \end{aligned}$$

Where each $T_i\,[\mathbf{D}_1, \ldots, \mathbf{D}_n]$ is some expression built out of $\mathbf{D}_1, \ldots, \mathbf{D}_n$ and finite or standard domains using the domain constructors →, ×, *, + described above. The example we met in 3.3.2. was

State = **Memory × Input × Output**
Memory = **Ide→[Value + {unbound}]**
Input = **Value***
Output = **Value***
Value = **Num + Bool + Proc**
Proc = **State→[State + {error}]**

An example of a single domain equation is the domain $\mathbf{D}^w$ of infinite sequences of members of **D** defined by:

$$\mathbf{D}^w = [\mathbf{D} \times \mathbf{D}^w]$$

If $\mathbf{s}\varepsilon\mathbf{D}^w$ then $\mathbf{s} = (\mathbf{d}_1, \mathbf{s}_1)\varepsilon[\mathbf{D} \times \mathbf{D}^w]$ where $\mathbf{s}_1 = (\mathbf{d}_2, \mathbf{s}_2)\varepsilon[\mathbf{D} \times \mathbf{D}^w]$ where $\mathbf{s}_2 = (\mathbf{d}_3, \mathbf{s}_3)\varepsilon[\mathbf{D} \times \mathbf{D}^w]$ ... i.e. $\mathbf{s} = (\mathbf{d}_1, (\mathbf{d}_2, (\mathbf{d}_3, \ldots)))$.

3.4. Functions

The word "function" has a number of different meanings which, if not carefully distinguished, can lead to total confusion. It is especially important to distinguish mathematical functions from the so called "functions" which occur as constructs in several programming languages (for example PASCAL, LISP and POP-2).

(i) A mathematical function $\mathbf{f}$ with *source* $\mathbf{A}$ and *target* $\mathbf{B}$ (which we write $\mathbf{f}: \mathbf{A} \rightarrow \mathbf{B}$) is a set of pairs $(\mathbf{a}, \mathbf{b}) \varepsilon \mathbf{A} \times \mathbf{B}$ such that if $(\mathbf{a}, \mathbf{b}_1) \varepsilon \mathbf{f}$ and $(\mathbf{a}, \mathbf{b}_2) \varepsilon \mathbf{f}$ then $\mathbf{b}_1 = \mathbf{b}_2$. If $(\mathbf{a}, \mathbf{b}) \varepsilon \mathbf{f}$ we write $\mathbf{f}\,\mathbf{a} = \mathbf{b}$ and thus $\mathbf{f} = \{(\mathbf{a}, \mathbf{f}\,\mathbf{a}) \mid \mathbf{a} \varepsilon \mathbf{A}\}$. In the notation $\mathbf{f}: \mathbf{A} \rightarrow \mathbf{B}$ the expression "$\mathbf{A} \rightarrow \mathbf{B}$" is called the *type* of $\mathbf{f}$ and denotes the set of all functions from $\mathbf{A}$ to $\mathbf{B}$.

(ii) A 'function' in a programming language like PASCAL is a *construct* which describes a *rule* for transforming an argument—the actual parameter—to a result.

Now if $\mathbf{F}$ is a function construct (as in (ii)) then one can associate with it a mathematical function $\mathbf{f}$: { actual parameters}→{results} defined by

$$\mathbf{fx} = \text{result of calling } \mathbf{F} \text{ on parameter } \mathbf{x}.$$

Indeed a simple denotational semantics might give $\mathbf{f}$ as the denotation of $\mathbf{F}$ (i.e. $\mathbf{F}[\![\mathbf{F}]\!] = \mathbf{f}$). However note that:

(a) Many *different* function constructs can denote the same mathematical function (for example different algorithms for sorting a list).

(b) A function construct is a *finite* object, whereas a mathematical function is typically an *infinite* set—for example the factorial function is the infinite set

$$\{(\mathbf{0}, \mathbf{1}), (\mathbf{1}, \mathbf{1}), (\mathbf{2}, \mathbf{2}), (\mathbf{3}, \mathbf{6}), (\mathbf{4}, \mathbf{24}), \ldots\}$$

(c) As we shall see later, except in simple cases, it will not be satisfactory to take the denotation of a function construct to be the mathematical function defined by its input/output behaviour. To handle side-effects, jumps out of the functions body, etc., we will need more complicated denotations.

Unless the contrary is clear from context the word "function" in this book means "mathematical function".

We shall use two main techniques for defining functions:

(i) λ-notation (see 3.4.1.).

(ii) Definition by recursion (see 3.4.9.).

3.4.1. λ-notation

3.4.1.1. Basic idea

Suppose E[**x**] is some expression involving **x** such that whenever **d**ε**D** is substituted for **x**—and we shall denote the result of such a substitution by E[**d**]—the resulting expression (namely E[**d**]) denotes a member of **D**′. For example, if both **D** and **D**′ are **Num**, then E[**x**] could be **x** + **1** (so E[**5**] = **5** + **1** = **6**) or perhaps **x** × **x** (then E[**5**] = **5** × **5** = **25**). For such expressions the notation:

$$\lambda \mathbf{x}\,.\,E[\mathbf{x}]$$

denotes the function **f: D→D**′ such that:

$$\text{for all } \mathbf{d}\varepsilon\mathbf{D}\text{: } \mathbf{fd} = E[\mathbf{d}]$$

For example:

(i) λ**x . x + 1** denotes the successor function of type **Num→Num**.
(ii) λ**x . x × x** denotes the squaring function of type **Num→Num**.
(iii) λ**x . (x = 0)→true, false** denotes the test-for-zero functions of type **Num→Bool**.

An expression of the form λ**x** . E[**x**] is called a *λ-expression,* **x** is its *bound variable* and E[**x**] its body.

This is the central idea of λ-notation; the various elaborations described below are just to make the descriptions of complicated functions a bit more intelligible.

N.B. The body of a λ-expression always extends as far to the right as possible, thus λ**x . x + 1** is λ**x . (x + 1)** not **(**λ**x . x) + 1**.

3.4.1.2. Elaborations

3.4.1.2.1. Explicitly indicating source and/or target

Sometimes it is not clear what the source (**D** say) or target (**D**′ say) of a function defined by a λ-expression are—for example consider λ**x . x**—in such cases one can, if necessary, indicate the desired information by writing **:D→D**′ after the λ-expression. For example λ**x . x: Num→Num**, λ**x . x: Bool→Bool**, λ**x . x + 1: Num→Num** etc.

Often the target but not the source is clear; in such cases one can write **:D** after the bound variable. For example λ**x:Num . x**, λ**x:Bool . x**, λ**x:Num . x + 1** etc.

3.4.1.2.2. More than one argument

If E[$\mathbf{x}_1$, ..., $\mathbf{x}_n$] is an expression having a value in **D′** when $\mathbf{x}_1 \varepsilon \mathbf{D}_1$, ..., $\mathbf{x}_n \varepsilon \mathbf{D}_n$ then the notation

$$\lambda(\mathbf{x}_1, \ldots, \mathbf{x}_n) \,.\, \mathrm{E}[\mathbf{x}_1, \ldots, \mathbf{x}_n]$$

is used to describe the function $\mathbf{f}$: $[\mathbf{D}_1 \times \ldots \times \mathbf{D}_n] \rightarrow \mathbf{D}'$ such that:

$$\text{for all } \mathbf{d}_1 \varepsilon \mathbf{D}_1, \ldots, \mathbf{d}_n \varepsilon \mathbf{D}_n\text{: } \mathbf{f}(\mathbf{d}_1, \ldots, \mathbf{d}_n) = \mathrm{E}[\mathbf{d}_1, \ldots, \mathbf{d}_n]$$

Examples are:

(i) $\lambda(\mathbf{x}_1,\mathbf{x}_2) \,.\, \mathbf{x}_1 + \mathbf{x}_2$; the addition function of type

$$[\mathbf{Num} \times \mathbf{Num}] \rightarrow \mathbf{Num}$$

(ii) $\lambda(\mathbf{x}_1,\mathbf{x}_2) \,.\, \mathbf{x}_1 < \mathbf{x}_2 \rightarrow \mathbf{error}, \mathbf{x}_1 - \mathbf{x}_2$; the subtraction function of type

$$[\mathbf{Num} \times \mathbf{Num}] \rightarrow [\mathbf{Num} + \{\mathbf{error}\}]$$

This notation for more than one argument can be combined with explicit indication of source on target, for example

$$\lambda(\mathbf{x}_1, \mathbf{x}_2) \,.\, \mathbf{x}_1 + \mathbf{x}_2 \text{: } [[\mathbf{Num} \times \mathbf{Num}] \rightarrow \mathbf{Num}]$$
$$\text{or } \lambda(\mathbf{x}_1, \mathbf{x}_2)\text{: } [\mathbf{Num} \times \mathbf{Num}] \,.\, \mathbf{x}_1 + \mathbf{x}_2$$

Functions like this can either be thought of as having many arguments or, perhaps more elegantly, as having just one argument which is a tuple.

3.4.1.3. Applying λ-expressions to arguments

Just as we can form expressions like "**f1**" to denote the application of **f** to **1** so we can from expressions in which λ-expressions are applied to arguments, for example:

$$(\lambda \mathbf{x} \,.\, \mathbf{x} + 1)\, 2 = 2 + 1 = 3$$
$$(\lambda(\mathbf{x},\mathbf{y}) \,.\, \mathbf{x} + \mathbf{y})\, (2,3) = 2 + 3 = 5$$

When 'evaluating' (λ**x** . E[**x**])**a** to E[**a**] one must only substitute **a** for those occurrences of **x** in E[**x**] which are *not* bound by inner λ's. For example **(λx . (λx . x))a** evaluates to **λx . x**, not **λx . a**.

3.4.1.4. Changing bound variables

The meaning of a λ-expression does not depend on the names of its bound variables—**λx . x + 1**, **λn . n + 1**, **λm . m + 1** all denote the same function. In general, bound variables can be renamed as long as the new name does not occur elsewhere in the λ-expression. If the new name does occur elsewhere then 'variable capture' may result and the meaning of the λ-expression change. An example of variable capture occurs if we rename **x** in **λx . (λy . x)** to **y** to get **λy . (λy . y)**—here the **x** is initially bound by the outer λ but after being renamed to **y** gets 'captured' by the inner λ and this capturing changes the meaning, thus:

$$((\lambda x . (\lambda y . x))1)\,2 = (\lambda y . 1)\,2 = 1$$
$$((\lambda y . (\lambda y . y))1)\,2 = (\lambda y . y)\,2 = 2$$

It is quite tricky (but not really difficult) to spell out exactly the general conditions under which variables get captured (see [Stoy]) but fortunately it is usually obvious in particular cases.

3.4.2. Higher order functions

The example in the previous section—**λx . (λy . x)**—is an example of a λ-expression which denotes a *higher order* function. Higher order functions are functions whose source or target contains functions. Thus **λx . (λy . x)** has a type of the form $D_1 \rightarrow [D_2 \rightarrow D_1]$ and so the result of applying **λx . (λy . x)** to an argument, d_1 say, is a member of $[D_2 \rightarrow D_1]$ ($\lambda y . d_1$ to be exact), i.e., a function.

Another example of a higher order function is

$$\textbf{twice}: [[\text{Num} \rightarrow \text{Num}] \rightarrow [\text{Num} \rightarrow \text{Num}]]$$

defined by **twice f = λx . f(fx)** (i.e. **twice = λf . (λx . f(fx))**). **twice f** is a function which does **f** twice, for example **twice (λn . n + 1)** is a function which applies **λn . n + 1** twice—i.e. adds **1** twice—i.e. adds **2**. Thus **twice (λn . n + 1) = λx . x + 2**, which can be verified formally as follows:

$$\begin{aligned}\mathbf{twice}\ (\lambda \mathbf{n}\,.\,\mathbf{n}+1) &= \lambda \mathbf{x}\,.\,(\lambda \mathbf{n}\,.\,\mathbf{n}+1)\ ((\lambda \mathbf{n}\,.\,\mathbf{n}+1)\ \mathbf{x})\\ &= \lambda \mathbf{x}\,.\,(\lambda \mathbf{n}\,.\,\mathbf{n}+1)\ (\mathbf{x}+1)\\ &= \lambda \mathbf{x}\,.\,(\mathbf{x}+1)+1\\ &= \lambda \mathbf{x}\,.\,\mathbf{x}+2\end{aligned}$$

Higher order functions are very useful and we shall frequently use them; for example the semantic functions for TINY were higher order— $\mathcal{C}$: **Com→[State→[State+{error}]]** so $\mathcal{C}$**[E]** (the result of applying $\mathcal{C}$ to **E**) is a function. Higher order functions are perfectly ordinary and everything we say about functions in general applies to them also. The reason why we singled them out for discussion is because in many programming languages (for example ALGOL 60 and PASCAL) 'functions' (as opposed to mathematical functions) are subject to various constraints. For example in neither ALGOL 60 nor PASCAL can 'functions' return 'functions' as results (so **twice** could not be programmed). These constraints are to enable efficient implementations of the languages and do not reflect anything inherent in the concept of a function. Indeed other (less efficient) languages like LISP or POP-2 allow the unrestricted programming of higher order 'functions'. As discussed earlier (at the beginning of 3.4.) one must be careful not to confuse the mathematical concept of a function with the various 'functions' occurring in programming languages.

3.4.3. Important notational conventions on precedence and association

(i) $\mathbf{f\,x_1 x_2 ... x_n}$ means $\mathbf{(...((f x_1) x_2)...)}$. For example, **f g x** means **(f g)x** *not* **f(g x)**. Thus application associates to the left.

(ii) $\mathbf{f;x_1;x_2;...;x_n}$ means $\mathbf{f(x_1\,(x_2\,(...(x_{n-1}\ x_n)...)))}$. For example, **f;g;x** means **f(g x)** *not* **(f g)x**. Thus ";" denotes application but unlike juxtaposition associates to the right.

(iii) $\mathbf{f_1\,x_{1\,1}...x_{1\,n};f_2\,x_{2\,1}...x_{2\,n};...;f_n\,x_{n\,1}...x_{nn}}$ means $\mathbf{(f_1 x_{1\,1}...x_{1\,n});(f_2 x_{2\,1}...x_{2\,n});...;(f_n x_{n\,1}...x_{nn})}$. For example, **f g;x** means **(f g); x** i.e. **(f g) x** and **f;g x** means **f;(g x)** i.e. **f(g x)**. Thus ";" binds more weakly than ordinary application (as denoted by juxtaposition).

(iv) $\lambda x_1 x_2 \ldots x_n . E[x_1, x_2, \ldots, x_n]$ means $\lambda x_1 . (\lambda x_2 . \ldots (\lambda x_n . E[x_1, x_2, \ldots, x_n]) \ldots)$. This notation can be extended to functions which take tuples as arguments; thus, for example, $\lambda x_1 (x_2,x_3) x_4 . E[x_1,x_2,x_3,x_4]$ means $\lambda x_1 . (\lambda (x_2,x_3) . (\lambda x_4 . E[x_1,x_2,x_3,x_4]))$.

(v) Conventions (i) and (iv) cooperate nicely; for example

$$(\lambda x_1 x_2 \ldots x_n . E[x_1,x_2,\ldots,x_n]) d_1 d_2 \ldots d_n = E[d_1,d_2,\ldots,d_n]$$

(vi) $D_1 \rightarrow D_2 \rightarrow \ldots \rightarrow D_n$ means $[D_1 \rightarrow [D_2 \rightarrow [\ldots [D_{n-1} \rightarrow D_n] \ldots]]]$ (see 3.3.3.3.).

(vii) The body of a λ-expression always extends as far to the right as possible, for example, $\lambda x . f x y z$ means $\lambda x . (f x y z)$ not $(\lambda x . f) x y z$.

3.4.4. Currying

Consider the two functions **plus** and **plusc** defined below:

(i) **plus: [Num × Num]→Num** , **plus =λ(n, m) . n+m**
(ii) **plusc: Num→Num→Num** , **plusc=λnm . n+m**

These functions are related in that **plus (n, m) = plusc n m**. It will often be convenient to use higher order functions like **plusc** which take their arguments 'one at a time' instead of **plus** which takes a pair (or more generally an n-tuple) as an argument. The advantage of **plusc** is that it can be applied to just one argument. For example, **plusc 1** is a well-formed expression denoting the function λ**m . 1 + m**; **plusc 2** denotes λ**m . 2 + m**, etc., but **plus 1**, **plus 2** do not make sense as **1**, **2** are not in the source **[Num × Num]** of **plus**. Another example is the semantic functions of TINY; because **C** has the type shown,

$$\mathcal{C}\text{: Com} \rightarrow \text{State} \rightarrow [\text{State} + \{\text{error}\}]$$

we can use **C[C]** to denote the denotation of **C**; if **C** had type **[Com × State]→[State + {error}]**, this expression would not make sense and we would have to use λ**s . C[C, s]**.
Functions of more than one argument which take them 'one at a time' like **plusc** and **C** are called *curried* (after Mr. Curry). In general if $f: [D_1 \times D_2 \times \ldots \times D_n] \rightarrow D$ then there is an equivalent curried function, **curry f**, say, of type $D_1 \rightarrow D_2 \rightarrow \ldots \rightarrow D_n \rightarrow D$, defined by

$$\mathbf{curry\ f} = \lambda \mathbf{x}_1 \mathbf{x}_2 \ldots \mathbf{x}_n \,.\, \mathbf{f}(\mathbf{x}_1, \mathbf{x}_2, \ldots, \mathbf{x}_n)$$

curry is itself a higher order function defined by

$$\mathbf{curry}: [[\mathbf{D}_1 \times \mathbf{D}_2 \times \ldots \times \mathbf{D}_n] \to \mathbf{D}] \to [\mathbf{D}_1 \to \mathbf{D}_2 \to \ldots \to \mathbf{D}_n \to \mathbf{D}]$$
$$\mathbf{curry} = \lambda \mathbf{f}\ \mathbf{x}_1 \mathbf{x}_2 \ldots \mathbf{x}_n \,.\, \mathbf{f}(\mathbf{x}_1, \mathbf{x}_2, \ldots, \mathbf{x}_n)$$

For example: $\mathbf{curry\ plus} = (\lambda \mathbf{f}\ \mathbf{x}_1 \mathbf{x}_2 \,.\, \mathbf{f}(\mathbf{x}_1, \mathbf{x}_2))\ \mathbf{plus}$

$$= (\lambda \mathbf{f} \,.\, (\lambda \mathbf{x}_1 \mathbf{x}_2 \,.\, \mathbf{f}(\mathbf{x}_1, \mathbf{x}_2)))\ \mathbf{plus}$$
$$= \lambda \mathbf{x}_1 \mathbf{x}_2 \,.\, \mathbf{plus}\ (\mathbf{x}_1, \mathbf{x}_2)$$
$$= \lambda \mathbf{x}_1 \mathbf{x}_2 \,.\, \mathbf{x}_1 + \mathbf{x}_2$$
$$= \mathbf{plusc}$$

There is an inverse to **curry** called **uncurry** defined by

$$\mathbf{uncurry}: [\mathbf{D}_1 \to \mathbf{D}_2 \to \ldots \to \mathbf{D}_n \to \mathbf{D}] \to [[\mathbf{D}_1 \times \mathbf{D}_2 \times \ldots \times \mathbf{D}_n] \to \mathbf{D}]$$
$$\mathbf{uncurry} = \lambda \mathbf{f}(\mathbf{x}_1, \mathbf{x}_2, \ldots, \mathbf{x}_n) \,.\, \mathbf{f}\ \mathbf{x}_1 \mathbf{x}_2 \ldots \mathbf{x}_n$$

The reader might like to show that **uncurry plusc = plus** and that for all **f**, **f′** of the appropriate types **curry (uncurry f) = f** and **uncurry (curry f′) = f′**.

3.4.5. Conditionals

A very important standard function is the conditional **cond** defined by

$$\mathbf{cond}: [\mathbf{D} \times \mathbf{D}] \to \mathbf{Bool} \to \mathbf{D} \qquad (\mathbf{D}\text{ arbitrary})$$

$$\mathbf{cond}\ (\mathbf{d}_1, \mathbf{d}_2)\ \mathbf{b} = \begin{cases} \mathbf{d}_1 & \text{if } \mathbf{b} = \mathbf{true} \\ \mathbf{d}_2 & \text{if } \mathbf{b} = \mathbf{false} \end{cases}$$

We use the following notations:

(i) $\mathbf{b} \to \mathbf{d}_1, \mathbf{d}_2$ means $\mathbf{cond}\ (\mathbf{d}_1, \mathbf{d}_2)\ \mathbf{b}$

(ii) $\mathbf{b}_1 \to \mathbf{d}_1, \mathbf{b}_2 \to \mathbf{d}_2, \ldots, \mathbf{b}_n \to \mathbf{d}_n, \mathbf{d}_{n+1}$ means $\mathbf{b}_1 \to \mathbf{d}_1, (\mathbf{b}_2 \to \mathbf{d}_2, (\ldots(\mathbf{b}_n \to \mathbf{d}_n, \mathbf{d}_{n+1})\ldots))$. If $\mathbf{b}_1, \ldots, \mathbf{b}_n$ are exhaustive we may omit $\mathbf{d}_{n+1}$ and write $\mathbf{b}_1 \to \mathbf{d}_1, \ldots, \mathbf{b}_n \to \mathbf{d}_n$.

Strictly speaking there is a conditional function, **condD** say, for each domain **D**. Thus **CondNum: [Num × Num]→Bool→Num** is different from **condIde: [Ide × Ide]→Bool→Ide** etc. In practice when we write $\mathbf{b} \to \mathbf{d}_1, \mathbf{d}_2$ it should be clear from context which domain is intended.

An important property of conditionals is: **(b→f, g) x = b→fx, gx.** Here,

f, **g** must have types of the form $\mathbf{D_1 \to D_2}$, so the left hand conditional has type $[[\mathbf{D_1 \to D_2}] \times [\mathbf{D_1 \to D_2}]] \to \mathbf{Bool} \to [\mathbf{D_1 \to D_2}]$ and the right hand conditional has type $[\mathbf{D_2} \times \mathbf{D_2}] \to \mathbf{Bool} \to \mathbf{D_2}$. Using **cond** instead of $\to$ we have: $\mathbf{cond}\,[\mathrm{D}_1 \to \mathrm{D}_2]\,(\mathbf{f},\mathbf{g})\,\mathbf{b}\,\mathbf{x} = \mathbf{cond}\,\mathrm{D}_2\,(\mathbf{f\,x},\,\mathbf{g\,x})\,\mathbf{b}$.

3.4.6. Cases notation

We shall illustrate cases notation with a couple of examples and hope the reader gets the general idea from these.

Suppose $\mathbf{D} = [\mathbf{Value} \times \mathbf{State}] + \{\mathbf{error}\}$ and $\mathbf{d} \varepsilon \mathbf{D}$ then the expression:

$$(\mathbf{d} = (\mathbf{v},\,\mathbf{s})) \to \mathrm{E}_1[\mathbf{v},\,\mathbf{s}],$$
$$(\mathbf{d} = \mathbf{error}) \to \mathrm{E}_2$$

means if **d** corresponds to a member **(v,s)** of **[Value × State]** then $\mathrm{E}_1[\mathbf{v},\mathbf{s}]$ else if **d** = **error** then E_2

As another example, suppose

$$\begin{aligned} \mathbf{D} &= \mathbf{D}_1 + \mathbf{D}_2 + \mathbf{D}_3 \\ \mathbf{D}_1 &= \mathbf{D}_{1\,1} \times \mathbf{D}_{1\,2} \\ \mathbf{D}_2 &= \{\mathbf{d}_2\} \\ \mathbf{D}_3 &= \mathbf{D}_{3\,1} \times \mathbf{D}_{3\,2} \times \mathbf{D}_{3\,3} \end{aligned}$$

Then the expression:

$$(\mathbf{d} = (\mathbf{d}_{1\,1},\,\mathbf{d}_{1\,2})) \to \mathrm{E}_1[\mathbf{d}_{1\,1},\,\mathbf{d}_{1\,2}],$$
$$(\mathbf{d} = \mathbf{d}_2) \to \mathrm{E}_2,$$
$$(\mathbf{d} = (\mathbf{d}_{3\,1},\,\mathbf{d}_{3\,2},\,\mathbf{d}_{3\,3})) \to \mathrm{E}_3[\mathbf{d}_{3\,1},\,\mathbf{d}_{3\,2},\,\mathbf{d}_{3\,3}],\ \mathrm{E}_4$$

means if **d** corresponds to $(\mathbf{d}_{1\,1},\ \mathbf{d}_{1\,2}) \varepsilon \mathbf{D}_1$ then $\mathrm{E}_1[\mathbf{d}_{1\,1},\ \mathbf{d}_{1\,2}]$; if **d** corresponds to $\mathbf{d}_2 \varepsilon \mathbf{D}_2$ then E_2; if **d** corresponds to $(\mathbf{d}_{3\,1},\ \mathbf{d}_{3\,2},\ \mathbf{d}_{3\,3}) \varepsilon \mathbf{D}_3$ then $\mathrm{E}_3[\mathbf{d}_{3\,1},\ \mathbf{d}_{3\,2},\ \mathbf{d}_{3\,3}]$; else E_4. This second cases statement is equivalent to

$$\mathbf{isD}_1\mathbf{d} \to (\lambda(\mathbf{d}_{1\,1},\,\mathbf{d}_{1\,2})\,.\,\mathrm{E}_1[\mathbf{d}_{1\,1},\,\mathbf{d}_{1\,2}])\,(\mathbf{outD}_1\,\mathbf{d}),$$
$$\mathbf{isD}_2\mathbf{d} \to \mathrm{E}_2,$$
$$\mathbf{isD}_3\mathbf{d} \to (\lambda(\mathbf{d}_{3\,1},\,\mathbf{d}_{3\,2},\,\mathbf{d}_{3\,3})\,.\,\mathrm{E}_3[\mathbf{d}_{3\,1},\,\mathbf{d}_{3\,2},\,\mathbf{d}_{3\,3}])\,(\mathbf{outD}_3\,\mathbf{d}),\ \mathrm{E}_4$$

This shows that cases notation both tests values and binds their components to variables. Examples of the use of cases notation are the semantic clauses for TINY above.

3.4.7. Updating functions

If $\mathbf{f}: \mathbf{D} \to \mathbf{D}'$, $\mathbf{d}_1, \ldots, \mathbf{d}_n \varepsilon \mathbf{D}$ and $\mathbf{d}_1', \ldots, \mathbf{d}_n' \varepsilon \mathbf{D}'$ then $\mathbf{f}[\mathbf{d}_1', \ldots, \mathbf{d}_n'/\mathbf{d}_1, \ldots, \mathbf{d}_n]$ denotes the function identical to **f** except at $\mathbf{d}_1, \ldots, \mathbf{d}_n$ where it has values $\mathbf{d}_1', \ldots, \mathbf{d}_n'$ respectively. Thus:

$$\begin{aligned}\mathbf{f}[\mathbf{d}_1', \ldots, \mathbf{d}_n'/\mathbf{d}_1, \ldots, \mathbf{d}_n] = \lambda \mathbf{d}\,.\, & \mathbf{d} = \mathbf{d}_1 \to \mathbf{d}_1', \\ & \mathbf{d} = \mathbf{d}_2 \to \mathbf{d}_2', \\ & \quad \vdots \\ & \mathbf{d} = \mathbf{d}_n \to \mathbf{d}_n', \mathbf{fd}.\end{aligned}$$

3.4.8. Generic functions

Functions like **cond** which, strictly speaking, are collections of functions, one for each domain of an appropriate type, are called *generic*. Other examples are **curry** and **uncurry**. The actual functions which make up the collections of functions are called *instances;* thus **condNum**, **condIde** are instances of **cond,** etc. The expressions which describe the types of the instances of generic functions are called *generic types*. For example $[\mathbf{D} \times \mathbf{D}] \to \mathbf{Bool} \to \mathbf{D}$ is the generic type of **cond**; an instance of this type with $\mathbf{D} = \mathbf{Num}$ is $[\mathbf{Num} \times \mathbf{Num}] \to \mathbf{Bool} \to \mathbf{Num}$. The generic type of **curry** is $[[\mathbf{D}_1 \times \mathbf{D}_2 \times \ldots \times \mathbf{D}_n] \to \mathbf{D}] \to [\mathbf{D}_1 \to \mathbf{D}_2 \to \ldots \to \mathbf{D}_n \to \mathbf{D}]$; in **curry plus** (see 3.4.4) it is used at instance
$[[\mathbf{Num} \times \mathbf{Num}] \to \mathbf{Num}] \to [\mathbf{Num} \to \mathbf{Num} \to \mathbf{Num}]$.

3.4.9. Ways of defining functions (including recursion)

A typical definition of a function **f** has the form

$$\begin{aligned} \mathbf{f}(\mathbf{x}_1, \ldots, \mathbf{x}_n) &= E[\mathbf{x}_1, \ldots, \mathbf{x}_n] \\ \text{or } \mathbf{f}\ \mathbf{x}_1 \ldots \mathbf{x}_n &= E[\mathbf{x}_1, \ldots, \mathbf{x}_n] \text{ if } \mathbf{f} \text{ is curried}\end{aligned}$$

For example:

$$\begin{aligned} \mathbf{plus}\ (\mathbf{x}, \mathbf{y}) &= \mathbf{x} + \mathbf{y} \\ \mathbf{plusc}\ \mathbf{x}\ \mathbf{y} &= \mathbf{x} + \mathbf{y}\end{aligned}$$

An equivalent (and sometimes more convenient) way of writing such definitions is as

$$\mathbf{f} = \lambda(\mathbf{x}_1, \ldots, \mathbf{x}_n) \,.\, E[\mathbf{x}_1, \ldots, \mathbf{x}_n]$$
$$\text{or } \mathbf{f} = \lambda\mathbf{x}_1 \ldots \mathbf{x}_n \,.\, E[\mathbf{x}_1, \ldots, \mathbf{x}_n]$$

For example

$$\mathbf{plus} \;=\; \lambda(\mathbf{x}, \mathbf{y}) \,.\, \mathbf{x}+\mathbf{y}$$
$$\mathbf{plusc} \;=\; \lambda\mathbf{xy} \,.\, \mathbf{x}+\mathbf{y}$$

We shall often need to define functions *recursively;* for example, we might define **fact: Num→Num** thus:

$$\mathbf{fact\ n} \;=\; (\mathbf{n}=0) \rightarrow 1,\ \mathbf{n} \times \mathbf{fact}\,(\mathbf{n}\text{-}1)$$
$$\text{or } \mathbf{fact} \;=\; \lambda\mathbf{n} \,.\, (\mathbf{n}=0) \rightarrow 1,\ \mathbf{n} \times \mathbf{fact}\,(\mathbf{n}\text{-}1)$$

We also sometimes need to define several functions by *mutual recursion.* If we use λ-expressions (as in the second definition of **fact** above) then the general form of mutually recursive definitions is:

$$\begin{aligned} \mathbf{f}_1 &= E_1[\mathbf{f}_1, \ldots, \mathbf{f}_n] \\ \mathbf{f}_2 &= E_2[\mathbf{f}_1, \ldots, \mathbf{f}_n] \\ &\vdots \\ \mathbf{f}_n &= E_n[\mathbf{f}_1, \ldots, \mathbf{f}_n] \end{aligned}$$

where the $E_i[\mathbf{f}_1, \ldots, \mathbf{f}_n]$ are λ-expressions. For example, if $E[\mathbf{f}]$ is $\lambda\mathbf{n} \,.\, (\mathbf{n}=0) \rightarrow 1,\ \mathbf{n} \times \mathbf{f}(\mathbf{n}\text{-}1)$ then the second definition of **fact** above is: $\mathbf{fact} = E[\mathbf{fact}]$. We thus see **fact** is a 'fixed point' of the function $\lambda\mathbf{f} \,.\, E[\mathbf{f}]$ —i.e. $(\lambda\mathbf{f} \,.\, E[\mathbf{f}])\ \mathbf{fact} = \mathbf{fact}$. $\lambda\mathbf{f} \,.\, E[\mathbf{f}]$ has type **[Num→Num]→[Num→Num]** and its 'fixed point' **fact** has type **[Num→Num]**. If we introduce a generic function **fix** of type **[D→D]→D** defined intuitively by

$$\mathbf{fix\ f} = \text{the fixed point of } \mathbf{f}$$

then the recursive definition of **fact** can be written *non-recursively* as

$$\mathbf{fact} \;=\; \mathbf{fix}\,(\lambda\mathbf{f\,n} \,.\, (\mathbf{n}=0) \rightarrow 1,\ \mathbf{n} \times \mathbf{f}\,(\mathbf{n}\text{-}1))$$

here **fix** is used at the instance **D=[Num→Num]** of its generic type **[D→D]→D**.

The precise definition and mathematical analysis of the function **fix** constitute the "theory of fixed points", which was discussed in 3.2.1. We shall not use **fix** but will define things recursively instead.

3.4.10. Cancelling out variables

Consider the equation **fx = gx;** if this holds for all **x** then it follows that **f = g**. In general an equation like

$$\mathbf{f\,x_1 \ldots x_i \ldots x_n = (E[x_1, \ldots, x_i])\,x_{i+1} \ldots x_n}$$

can be simplified to

$$\mathbf{f\,x_1 \ldots x_i = E[x_1, \ldots, x_i]}$$

as long as $\mathbf{x_{i+1}, \ldots, x_n}$ do not occur in $\mathbf{E[x_1, \ldots, x_i]}$. A common example of such simplifications is with definitions like

$$\mathbf{f\,xy = px \rightarrow gxy,\ hxy}$$

Using the fact that **px→gxy, hxy = (px→gx, hx) y** we can reduce this equation to

$$\mathbf{f\,xy = (px \rightarrow gx,\ hx)\ y}$$

and then cancel **y** to get

$$\mathbf{f\,x = p\,x \rightarrow g\,x,\ h\,x}$$

Now the definition

$$\mathbf{f\,x_1 \ldots x_n = (E[x_1, \ldots, x_i])x_{i+1} \ldots x_n}$$

is equivalent to

$$\mathbf{f = \lambda x_1 \ldots x_n\ .\ (E[x_1, \ldots, x_i])\ x_{i+1} \ldots x_n}$$

and just as the first definition can be simplified to

$$\mathbf{f\,x_1 \ldots x_i = E[x_1, \ldots, x_i]}$$

so the second one can be simplified to

$$\mathbf{f = \lambda x_1 \ldots x_i\ .\ E[x_1, \ldots, x_i]}$$

In general $\mathbf{\lambda x_1 \ldots x_i \ldots x_n\ .\ (E[x_1, \ldots, x_i])\ x_{i+1} \ldots x_n}$ can be simplified to $\mathbf{\lambda x_1 \ldots x_i\ .\ E[x_1, \ldots, x_i]}$ as long as $\mathbf{x_{i+1}, \ldots, x_n}$ do not occur in $\mathbf{E[x_1. \ldots, x_i]}$. For example, λ**xy . px→gxy, hxy** can be simplified to λ**x . px→gx, hx**.

N.B. When using ";" (see 3.4.3.) one must be careful with cancelling. For example, if **fx = g;h;x** then it *does not* follow that **f = g;h**. Similarly, λ**x . g;h;x** *does not* simplify to **g;h**.

3.4.11. where notation

Sometimes it is convenient to 'structure' expressions by writing

$$\begin{aligned} E[\mathbf{x}_1, \ldots, \mathbf{x}_n] \ \mathbf{where}\ \mathbf{x}_1 &= E_1 \\ \mathbf{and}\quad \mathbf{x}_2 &= E_2 \\ \vdots \quad & \\ \mathbf{and}\quad \mathbf{x}_n &= E_n \end{aligned}$$

instead of $E[E_1, \ldots, E_n]$. For example

$$\begin{aligned} \mathbf{x}_1 \times \mathbf{x}_2 \ \mathbf{where}\ \mathbf{x}_1 &= \mathbf{2+3} \\ \mathbf{and}\quad \mathbf{x}_2 &= \mathbf{6\text{-}7} \end{aligned}$$

instead of **(2+3) × (6-7)**. Use of **where** can sometimes shorten expressions and highlight essential aspects of their structure; for example

$$\begin{aligned} \mathbf{C[C_1;\, C_2]s} &= \mathbf{(s' = error) \to error,\ C[C_2]s'} \\ \mathbf{where\ s'} &= \mathbf{C[C_1]s} \end{aligned}$$

One can also use **where** for 'subsidiary' functions, for example

$$\mathbf{(f1) + (f2)\ where\ fx = x \times x}$$

which means $\mathbf{((\lambda x\,.\,x \times x)1) + ((\lambda x\,.\,x \times x)2) = 5}$

If the subsidiary function is recursive, we draw attention to that fact by using "**whererec**" instead of "**where**". For example

$$\mathbf{fact\ 6\ whererec\ fact\ n = (n=0) \to 1,\ n \times fact\,(n\text{-}1)}$$

If several subsidiary functions are to be mutually recursive then we write

$$\begin{aligned} E[\mathbf{f}_1, \ldots, \mathbf{f}_n]\ \mathbf{whererec}\ \mathbf{f}_1 &= E_1[\mathbf{f}_1, \ldots, \mathbf{f}_n] \\ &\ \vdots \\ \mathbf{and}\ \mathbf{f}_n &= E_n[\mathbf{f}_1, \ldots, \mathbf{f}_n] \end{aligned}$$

(here we assume the subsidiary functions are being defined as λ-expressions, but this is not necessary).

3.4.12. Composition and sequencing

3.4.12.1 Composition

If **f**: $\mathbf{D_1 \to D_2}$ and **g**: $\mathbf{D_2 \to D_3}$ then their *composition* $\mathbf{g \circ f}$: $\mathbf{D_1 \to D_3}$ is defined by $\mathbf{g \circ f = \lambda x . g(f\,x)}$. Notice that in $\mathbf{g \circ f}$, **f** is 'done first'..

3.4.12.2. Sequencing

We are going to define **f★g** where **f** and **g** have a variety of types. Before giving exact details, here is the essential idea: **f★g** is the function corresponding to first doing **f**; if **f** produces an error then **error** is the result of **f★g**; otherwise the results of **f** are 'fed to' **g**. **f★g** is like $\mathbf{g \circ f}$ except that

(i) Errors are propagated.
(ii) **g** may be curried.

Here now are the cases we shall need:

(a) Suppose **f**: $\mathbf{D_1 \to [D_2 + \{error\}]}$ and **g**: $\mathbf{D_2 \to [D_3 + \{error\}]}$; then **f★g**: $\mathbf{D_1 \to [D_3 + \{error\}]}$ is defined by:

$$\mathbf{f \star g = \lambda x . fx = error \to error, g(fx)}$$

(b) Suppose **f**: $\mathbf{D_1 \to [[D_2 \times D_3] + \{error\}]}$ and **g**: $\mathbf{D_2 \to D_3 \to [D_4 + \{error\}]}$ then **f★g**: $\mathbf{D_1 \to [D_4 + \{error\}]}$ is defined by:

$$\mathbf{f \star g = \lambda x . (f\,x = error) \to error, (f\,x = (d_2, d_3)) \to g\, d_2 d_3}$$

To see the use of ★ observe that the semantic clause:

$$\mathcal{C}[\mathbf{C_1; C_2}]\,\mathbf{s} = (\mathcal{C}[\mathbf{C_1}]\,\mathbf{s} = \mathbf{error}) \to \mathbf{error}, \mathcal{C}[\mathbf{C_2}]\,(\mathcal{C}[\mathbf{C_1}]\,\mathbf{s})$$

can be simplified to

$$\mathcal{C}[\mathbf{C_1; C_2}] = \mathcal{C}[\mathbf{C_1}] \star \mathcal{C}[\mathbf{C_2}]$$

Here we have an example of case (a) with $\mathbf{D_1 = D_2 = D_3 = State}$. As another example the semantic clause

$$\begin{aligned} \mathcal{C}[\mathbf{output\ E}]\mathbf{s} = {} & (\mathcal{E}[\mathbf{E}]\,\mathbf{s} = \mathbf{error}) \to \mathbf{error}, \\ & (\mathcal{E}[\mathbf{E}]\mathbf{s} = (\mathbf{v,(m,i,o)})) \to (\mathbf{m,i,v\ .\ o}) \end{aligned}$$

can be simplified to

$$\mathbf{C[output\ E]} = \mathbf{E[E]} \bigstar \lambda \mathbf{v(m,i,o).(m,i,v.o)}$$

Here we have case (b) with $\mathbf{D_1 = D_3 = State}$, $\mathbf{D_2 = Value}$.

As a final example (again of case (b) with $\mathbf{D_1 = D_3 = State}$, $\mathbf{D_2 = Value}$) the semantic clause (E6) in 2.4.4.1. can be written:

$$\mathbf{E[E_1 = E_2]} = \mathbf{E[E_1]} \bigstar \lambda \mathbf{v_1 . E[E_2]} \bigstar \lambda \mathbf{v_2\ s.(v_1 = v_2, s)}$$

The reader is urged to ensure he follows these examples by expanding the ★'s. We shall also use $\mathbf{f} \bigstar \mathbf{g}$ when **f** cannot produce **error**. Case (a) then corresponds to $\mathbf{f} \bigstar \mathbf{g} = \mathbf{g} \circ \mathbf{f}$, and case (b) to $\mathbf{f} \bigstar \mathbf{g} = \mathbf{g} \circ \mathbf{(uncurry\ f)}$.

Finally, note that:

(i) ★ is associative, so expressions like $\mathbf{f} \bigstar \mathbf{g} \bigstar \mathbf{h}$ are unambiguous (since $\mathbf{f} \bigstar (\mathbf{g} \bigstar \mathbf{h}) = (\mathbf{f} \bigstar \mathbf{g}) \bigstar \mathbf{h}$).

(ii) Expressions like $\mathbf{f} \bigstar \mathbf{g} \bigstar \lambda \mathbf{x.h} \bigstar \mathbf{k}$ mean $\mathbf{f} \bigstar \mathbf{g} \bigstar (\lambda \mathbf{x.(h} \bigstar \mathbf{k}))$—see 3.4.3. (vii).

4. Denotational description of TINY

The purpose of the battery of abbreviatory conventions described in the preceding chapter is to provide a set of notations which are both powerful and concise. We would like the expressions and definitions we write—semantic clauses, for example—to be both brief and readable. Unfortunately there is some conflict between these two requirements—compact notations are often hard to understand, but, conversely, long descriptions often hide the really important facts in a confusing morass of minor detail. Exactly how to trade off compactness versus explicit detail is still a matter of controversy and the reader must decide for himself whether powerful abbreviations (like the sequencing operator ★ of 3.4.12.2. for example) are a help or hindrance to understanding.

In the rest of this chapter we describe TINY using the notations and concepts presented in chapter 3. We give the new version of the semantics without comment, but indicate previous sections which explain various notations when they are first used. The new semantics is completely equivalent to the one given in chapter 2 and so the explanations there apply here also.

4.1. Abstract syntax (see 3.1.)

4.1.1. Syntactic domains

E ranges over the domain **Exp** of expressions
C ranges over the domain **Com** of commands

4.1.2. Syntactic clauses

$\mathbf{E} ::= \mathbf{0} \mid \mathbf{1} \mid \mathbf{true} \mid \mathbf{false} \mid \mathbf{read} \mid \mathbf{I} \mid \mathbf{not}\ \mathbf{E} \mid \mathbf{E}_1 = \mathbf{E}_2 \mid \mathbf{E}_1 + \mathbf{E}_2$
$\mathbf{C} ::= \mathbf{I} := \mathbf{E} \mid \mathbf{output}\ \mathbf{E} \mid \mathbf{if}\ \mathbf{E}\ \mathbf{then}\ \mathbf{C}_1\ \mathbf{else}\ \mathbf{C}_2 \mid \mathbf{while}\ \mathbf{E}\ \mathbf{do}\ \mathbf{C} \mid \mathbf{C}_1 ; \mathbf{C}_2$

4.2. Semantics

4.2.1. Semantic domains (see 3.3.)

State = Memory × Input × Output
Memory = Ide→[Value + {unbound}]
Input = Value*
Output = Value*
Value = Num + Bool

4.2.2. Auxiliary functions (see 3.4.)

These functions are useful for 'factoring out' common parts of the semantic clauses in 4.2.4.

4.2.2.1. result

Informal description: **result v** is the denotation of an expression which returns **v** as its value and does not change the state.

Formal description: **result:Value→State→[[Value × State] + {error}]**
result = λv s . (v,s)

(see (iii) (a) in the comments at the end of 3.3.3.4.).

4.2.2.2. donothing

Informal description: **donothing** is the denotation of a command which has no effect.

Formal description: **donothing:State→[State + {error}]**
donothing = λs . s

4.2.2.3. checkNum

Informal description: **checkNum v** is the denotation of an expression which returns **v** and an unchanged state if **v**ε**Num** and **error** otherwise.

Formal description:

checkNum:Value→State→[[Value × State] + {error}]
checkNum = λv s . isNum v→(v,s), error

(see 3.3.3.4.).

4.2.2.4. checkBool

Informal description: **checkBool v** is the denotation of an expression which returns **v** and an unchanged state if **v**ε**Bool** and **error** otherwise.

Formal description:

checkBool:Value→State→[[Value × State] + {error}]
checkBool = λv s . isBool v→(v,s), error

4.2.3. Semantic functions

E:Exp→State→[[Value × State] + {error}]
C:Com→State→[State + {error}]

4.2.4. Semantic clauses

4.2.4.1. Clauses for expressions

(E1) **E[0] = result 0, E[1] = result 1**
(E2) **E[true] = result true, E[false] = result false**
(E3) **E[read] =**
λ(m,i,o) . null i→error, (hdi, (m, tli, o)) (see 3.3.3.3.)
(E4) **E[I] =**
λ(m,i,o) . m I = unbound→error, (m I, (m,i,o))
(E5) **E[not E] =**
E[E] ★ checkBool ★ λv . result (not v) (see 3.4.12.2.)
(E6) **E[E_1 = E_2] =**
E[E_1] ★ λv_1 . E[E_2] ★ λv_2 . result (v_1 = v_2)
(E7) **E[E_1 + E_2] =**
E[E_1] ★ checkNum ★ λv_1 . E[E_2] ★ checkNum ★ λv_2 . result (v_1 + v_2)

4.2.4.2. Clauses for commands

(C1) **C[I: = E] = E[E] ★ λv (m, i, o) . (m[v/I], i, o)**
(C2) **C[output E] = E[E] ★ λv (m, i, o) . (m, i, v . o)**
(C3) **C[if E then C_1 else C_2] =**
E[E] ★ checkBool ★ cond (C[C_1], C[C_2]) (see 3.4.5.)
(C4) **C[while E do C] =**
E[E]★checkBool★cond (C[C]★C[while E do C], donothing)
(C5) **C[C_1;C_2] = C[C_1] ★ C[C_2]**

5. Standard semantics

The description of TINY given in the last chapter was designed to illustrate the main ideas and notations of denotational semantics. For real languages (such as PASCAL or ALGOL 60) it is necessary to use rather more sophisticated denotations. In particular:

(i) Instead of denotations transforming states 'directly' it is necessary for them to transform states indirectly via *continuations* (see 5.1. below). This enables jumps to be handled.

(ii) The binding of identifiers to values needs to be split into two parts: a mapping from identifiers to 'variables' and a mapping from 'variables' to values. This enables sharing or aliasing to be handled.

A semantics based on (i) and (ii) is called a *standard semantics*. If we describe languages using fixed standard techniques then comparisons between languages are made easier. The disadvantage is that for any particular language the 'fit' of the techniques may not be perfect. For example, when we come to discuss the 'dynamic binding' of LISP, the two-stage binding of identifiers to values of (ii) is not completely appropriate—however the distortion it involves is compensated for by the ability to discuss very different languages (for example, PASCAL and LISP) within a single framework.

In this chapter we describe the central ideas and techniques of standard semantics. In the next chapter we illustrate these by giving a standard semantics of a slight extension of TINY called SMALL. Then, in the rest of the book we apply standard techniques to describe many different kinds of constructs (including most of those occurring in PASCAL and ALGOL 60).

5.1. Continuations

The development of *continuations* [Strachey and Wadsworth] was an important advance in the descriptive techniques of semantics. It led to:

(i) Simplification—both conceptual and notational—in the description of most constructs.

(ii) Smooth descriptions of various constructs which, previously, were impossible to handle (for example jumps back into already exited procedures, co-routines and 'state saving').

5.1.1. Modelling the 'rest of the program'

Most constructs can be thought of as transforming some input into some result— the exact type of these depending on the construct. In TINY the inputs to both commands and expressions are states; the results are states (or **error**) in the case of commands, and value/state pairs (or **error**) in the case of expressions.

In the kind of semantics described so far, each construct *directly* denotes its input/result transformation, and the transformation of a complete program is got (roughly) by combining (with ★) the transformations of its components. This type of semantics is called a *direct semantics.* It suffers from the problem that there is no way a construct can avoid passing its result to the rest of the program following it. If a construct produces an abnormal result, say **error**, then the rest of the program has to cope with this. Thus semantic clauses get cluttered up with tests for abnormal values. Although these tests can be hidden in operators like ★ the checking involved is unnatural—intuitively, when an error occurs the rest of the program is simply ignored and the computation just stops.

In a *continuation semantics* we make the denotations of constructs depend on the 'rest of the program'— or *continuation*—following them. The intuitive idea is that each construct decides for itself where to pass its result. Usually it will pass it to the continuation corresponding to the 'code' textually following it in the program—the *normal continuation*—but in some cases this will be ignored and the result passed to some other 'abnormal' continuation. For example:

(i) When an error occurs the normal continuation is ignored and control passes to a continuation corresponding to an error stop.

(ii) When a jump occurs the normal continuation is ignored and control passes to a continuation corresponding to the rest of the program following the label jumped to.

This is all very vague and probably will not be fully comprehensible until we have explained the formal details. Continuations can, at first, be a bit tricky and the reader should not worry if to start with everything seems back to front and unnaturally higher order—one needs to work through a few concrete examples before thinking with continuations comes naturally.

We now explain exactly what continuations are and which aspects of the 'rest of the program' they model. Formally, a continuation is a function from whatever the 'rest of the program' expects to be passed as an intermediate result—and this depends on what the 'rest of the program' follows— to the *final answer* of the program. For example in the TINY program **I: = E;C,** the intermediate result passed to the 'rest of the program' following **I: = E**—i.e. passed to **C**—is a state, and the final answer is a state or **error**; however the intermediate result passed to the 'rest of the program' following **E**—i.e. passed to **I: = ;C**—is a value (**E**'s value), together with a state (the state after doing **E**). The continuations corresponding to the first case—i.e. corresponding to the 'rest of the program' following a command— are called *command continuations* and form a domain **Cont** defined by

$$\text{Cont} = \text{State} \rightarrow [\text{State} + \{\text{error}\}]$$

command
continuations

results of   final
commands   answers

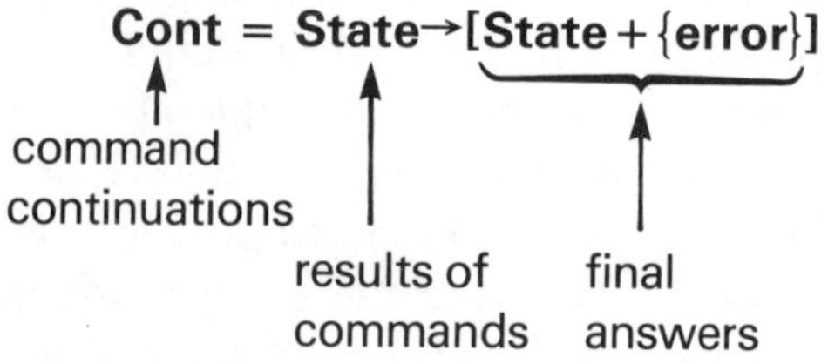

Continuations corresponding to the second case—i.e. corresponding to the 'rest of the program' following expressions—are called *expression continuations* and form a domain **Econt** defined by:

$$\text{Econt} = \text{Value} \rightarrow \text{State} \rightarrow [\text{State} + \{\text{error}\}]$$

expression
continuations

results of   final
expressions   answers
(curried)

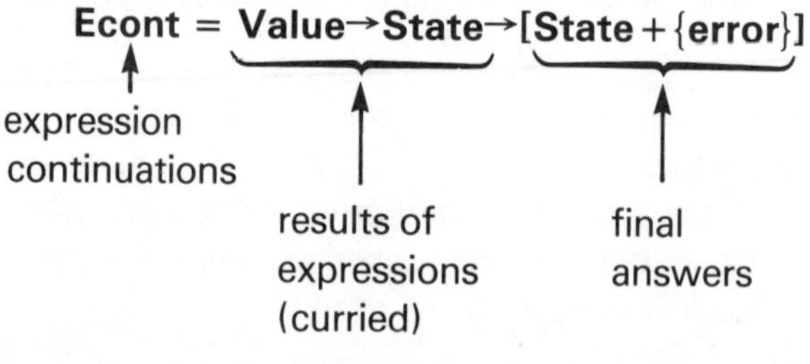

We define **Econt** as above rather than uncurried as
[Value × State]→**[State + {error}]**, so that **Econt = Value→Cont**—this turns out to be very convenient when we come to write semantic clauses.

We shall use **c**, **c**′, $\mathbf{c}_1$, $\mathbf{c}_2$, etc., for typical members of **Cont**; **k**, **k**′, $\mathbf{k}_1$, $\mathbf{k}_2$, etc., will be typical members of **Econt**. The continuations described above are appropriate for TINY but slightly too simple for general use. In 5.5. we describe domains **Cc** and **Ec** of *standard* command and expression continuations; however, for the time being, we shall continue to work with **Cont** and **Econt** since they embody the essential ideas without unnecessary extra detail.

5.1.2. Direct and continuation semantics

Recall that in our direct semantics of TINY (see 4) we used semantic functions with the following types:

$$\mathcal{E}:\mathbf{Exp}\rightarrow\mathbf{State}\rightarrow[[\mathbf{Value}\times\mathbf{State}]+\{\mathbf{error}\}]$$
$$\mathcal{C}:\mathbf{Com}\rightarrow\mathbf{State}\rightarrow[\mathbf{State}+\{\mathbf{error}\}]$$

In a *continuation semantics* the denotations of constructs are functions of continuations as well as of states. If we (temporarily) use $\mathcal{E}'$ and $\mathcal{C}'$ for the continuation semantic functions, then their types are:

$$\mathcal{E}':\mathbf{Exp}\rightarrow\mathbf{Econt}\rightarrow\mathbf{State}\rightarrow[\mathbf{State}+\{\mathbf{error}\}]$$
$$\text{(i.e. } \mathcal{E}':\mathbf{Exp}\rightarrow\mathbf{Econt}\rightarrow\mathbf{Cont}\text{)}$$
$$\mathcal{C}':\mathbf{Com}\rightarrow\mathbf{Cont}\rightarrow\mathbf{State}\rightarrow[\mathbf{State}+\{\mathbf{error}\}]$$
$$\text{(i.e. } \mathcal{C}':\mathbf{Com}\rightarrow\mathbf{Cont}\rightarrow\mathbf{Cont}\text{)}$$

and are defined so that:

$$\mathcal{E}'[\![\mathbf{E}]\!]\,\mathbf{k}\,\mathbf{s} = \begin{cases} \mathbf{k}\,\mathbf{v}\,\mathbf{s}' & \text{where } \mathbf{E} \text{ has value } \mathbf{v} \text{ and transforms } \mathbf{s} \text{ to } \mathbf{s}'. \\ \mathbf{error} & \text{otherwise.} \end{cases}$$

$$\mathcal{C}'[\![\mathbf{C}]\!]\,\mathbf{c}\,\mathbf{s} = \begin{cases} \mathbf{c}\,\mathbf{s}' & \text{if } \mathbf{C} \text{ transforms } \mathbf{s} \text{ to } \mathbf{s}' \\ \mathbf{error} & \text{otherwise} \end{cases}$$

Thus, in general, the continuation denotation of a construct is a function of a continuation and state which yields the final answer of the program—this final answer being obtained by passing some intermediate results (e.g. **v**, **s**′, etc.) to some continuation (i.e. to the 'rest of the program'). Normally this continuation will correspond to the program text following the construct, but sometimes other continuations are appropriate. For example, in the case of *jumps*—commands of the form **goto I**, say—the semantic clause will be roughly

$$\mathbf{C'[goto\ I]\,c\,s = c'\,s} \quad \text{where } \mathbf{c'} \text{ is some continuation specified by } \mathbf{I} \text{ (e.g. bound to } \mathbf{I} \text{ in } \mathbf{s}\text{)}$$

We shall discuss this kind of thing in detail later; however for the time being we concentrate on explaining what a continuation semantics just for TINY looks like. We start with identifiers.

The continuation semantic clause for identifiers is:

$$\mathbf{E'[I]\,k\,(m,i,o) = (m\,I = unbound) \rightarrow error,\ k(m\,I)(m,i,o)}$$

Thus the final answer yielded by **I** when the 'rest of the program' is **k** and the state is **(m,i,o)** is **error** if **I** is unbound in **m**, and otherwise is the final answer produced by **k** when it is passed **m I** and **(m,i,o)** as intermediate results. Notice how continuation semantics allows us to explicitly specify final answers—e.g. **error**—as well as intermediate results (e.g. **m I**). In the case that **m I** is **unbound** we ignore **k** and immediately stop with **error**. In a direct semantics one can only specify the intermediate results, and so **error** has to be an intermediate result with the consequence that messy operators like ★ are then needed to handle it. To see this more clearly, here is the semantic clause for $\mathbf{C_1;C_2}$:

$$\mathbf{C'[C_1;C_2]\,c\,s = C'[C_1]\,(C'[C_2]\,c)\,s}$$

This says we evaluate $\mathbf{C_1}$ with a continuation $\mathbf{C'[C_2]\,c}$ (i.e. a 'rest of the program' corresponding to $\mathbf{C_2}$ followed by **c**). Now if $\mathbf{C_1}$ generates an error then it can simply ignore its continuation $\mathbf{C'[C_2]\,c}$ and 'stop' with final answer **error**. In a direct semantics, denotations cannot choose to *not* send an intermediate result to the 'rest of the program'. One way of thinking of direct semantics is as a special kind of continuation semantics in which one is always forced to send some intermediate result to the normal (i.e. textual) continuation. This follows from the fact that one can prove (for TINY) that:

$$\text{for all } \mathbf{E \varepsilon Exp,\ k \varepsilon Econt{:}\ E'[E]\,k = E[E] \star k}$$
$$\text{for all } \mathbf{C \varepsilon Com,\ c \varepsilon Cont{:}\ C'[C]\,c = C[C] \star c}$$

For TINY this actually defines $\mathbf{E'}$ and $\mathbf{C'}$, but normally one has to write out semantic clauses for continuation semantic functions directly since there may be no direct semantics available. For example, it is rather hard (though not impossible) to define **C[goto I]** and to extend ★ so that **C′[goto I] c = C[goto I] ★ c**. The meaning of ★ (at least as defined in 3.4.12.2.) implies that if **C[goto I] s** is not **error** then **C[goto I]★c = c (C[goto I])**, so there is no way to avoid **c** getting some intermediate result passed to it. In other words, **C′[goto I] c = C[goto I] ★ c** is incompatible with **C′[goto I] c** ignoring **c**. By complicating ★ it is possible to get round this and to obtain a direct semantics of **goto I** (i.e. to concoct a definition of **C[goto I]** that works) but the details are messy and only of technical interest (see [Bjorner & Jones]). For languages in which the flow of control may fail to follow the textual structure of programs, the most natural description is a continuation semantics. From now on, all our semantics will use continuations and we shall drop the primes on continuation semantic functions.

5.1.3. Continuation semantics of TINY

In this section we illustrate the ideas just described by giving a continuation semantics of TINY.

5.1.3.1. Semantic domains and functions

Domains:

State	=	**Memory × Input × Output**
Memory	=	**Ide→[Value + {unbound}]**
Input	=	**Value***
Output	=	**Value***
Value	=	**Num + Bool**
Cont	=	**State→[State + {error}]**
Econt	=	**Value→Cont**

Functions:

E:Exp→Econt→Cont
C:Com→Cont→Cont

(we no longer use **E′** and **C′**)

5.1.3.2. Semantic clauses

Expressions:

(E1) **E[0] k s = k 0 s, E[1] k s = k 1 s**

Each numeral passes the appropriate number, together with an unchanged state, to the continuation. The state is unchanged since evaluating numerals has no side effects. Notice that by cancelling (see 3.4.10.) (E1) can be simplified to:

E[0] k = k 0 , E[1] k = k 1

(E2) **E[true] k = k true , E[false] k = k false**

(E3) **E[read] k (m,i,o) = null i→error , k (hd i) (m,tl i,o)**

If the input **i** is empty then the program stops with final answer **error;** otherwise **hd i** and the side-effected state **(m,tl i,o)** are passed as intermediate results to **k**.

(E4) **E[I] k (m,i,o) = (m I = unbound)→error , k (m I) (m,i,o)**

This was explained above.

(E5) **E[not E] k s = E[E] (λv s′ . isBool v→k (not v) s′ , error) s**

E is evaluated and the resulting value **v** and state **s′** are passed to the continuation **(λv s′ . isBool v→k (not v) s′, error)**. This continuation sends **not v** and **s′** to **k** if **v**ε**Bool;** otherwise **k** is ignored and the result is **error**. If we define **err** = **λs . error** then the techniques of 3.4.10 allow us to simplify (E5) to:

E[not E] k = E[E]λv . isBool v→k (not v), err

(E6) **E[E_1 = E_2] k = E[E_1] λv_1 . E[E_2] λv_2 . k(v_1 = v_2)**

We evaluate **E_1** to get **v_1**, which is then passed to **λv_1 . E[E_2]λv_2 . k(v_1 = v_2)**; this evaluates **E_2** to get **v_2** which is then passed to the continuation **λv_2 . k(v_1 = v_2)**, which passes **v_1 = v_2** to **k**. If **E_1** caused an error then its continuation would be ignored; for example

E[read = E] k (m,( ),o) = **E[read](...)(m,( ),o)**
= **error** (since **null ( ) = true**—see (E3))

(E7) $\mathbf{E[E_1 + E_2]\,k} =$

$$\mathbf{E[E_1]\lambda v_1 \,.\, E[E_2]\lambda v_2 \,.\, isNum\; v_1 \;and\; isNum\; v_2 \rightarrow k(v_1 + v_2),\; err}$$

err = λ**s . error**; thus $\mathbf{E_1}$ is evaluated to get $\mathbf{v_1}$; then $\mathbf{E_2}$ is evaluated to get $\mathbf{v_2}$; then if $\mathbf{v_1}$ and $\mathbf{v_2}$ are both numbers, $\mathbf{v_1 + v_2}$ is passed to **k**; otherwise **k** is ignored and **error** results.

Commands:

(C1) $\mathbf{C[I\!:=\!E]\,c = E[E]\lambda v(m,i,o)\,.\,c(m[v/I],i,o)}$

E is evaluated and its result passed to the continuation λ**v(m,i,o) . c(m[v/I],i,o)**, which passes **(m[v/I],i,o)** to **c**.

(C2) $\mathbf{C[output\; E]\,c = E[E]\lambda v(m,i,o)\,.\,c(m,i,v\,.\,o)}$

The value of **E** is put on to the front of the output component of the store and the result passed to **c**. Further discussion of output is given in the next section.

(C3) $\mathbf{C[if\; E\; then\; C_1\; else\; C_2]\,c} =$

$$\mathbf{E[E]\lambda v\,.\,isBool\; v \rightarrow (v \rightarrow C[C_1]\,c,\; C[C_2]\,c),\; err}$$

(C4) $\mathbf{C[while\; E\; do\; C]\,c} =$

$$\mathbf{E[E]\lambda v\,.\,isBool\; v \rightarrow (v \rightarrow C[C];\; C[while\; E\; do\; C]\,c,\; c),\; err}$$

As described in 3.4.3. (iii), **C[C]; C[while E do C] c** means **C[C](C[while E do C] c)**. Thus if **E**'s value is **true, C** is done and the resulting state passed back to **C[while E do C] c** ((C4) is recursive). If **v** is **false** then the state resulting from **E** is sent straight to **c**.

$$\begin{aligned}\text{Thus}\quad \mathbf{C[while\; false\; do\; C]\,c} &= \mathbf{E[false]\lambda v\,.\,isBool\; v \rightarrow (v \rightarrow \ldots,\; c),\; err}\\ &= \mathbf{(\lambda v\,.\,isBool\; v \rightarrow (v \rightarrow \ldots,\; c),\; err)\; false}\\ &= \mathbf{(false \rightarrow \ldots,\; c)}\\ &= \mathbf{c}\end{aligned}$$

so **while false do C** has no effect.

(C5) $\mathbf{C[C_1;C_2] = C[C_1] \circ C[C_2]}$

here $\circ$ is function composition (see 3.4.12.1.), so (C5) is equivalent to

$$\mathbf{C[C_1;C_2]\,c\,s = C[C_1]\,(C[C_2]\,c)\,s}$$

which we discussed above.

5.1.4. Final answers and output

In this section we point out, and correct, three inaccuracies which have crept into our semantics. These are:

5.1.4.1. Final answers are not states

In defining continuations we took the domain of final answers to be [**State** + {**error**}]. This is unnatural. In practice, the result of running a program is not thought of as the whole state but just the output (together with an indication of whether the program halted normally or via an error).

5.1.4.2. Output is not part of the state

By defining **State = Memory × Input × Output** we made the output file just as accessible to programs as the memory and input. Usually information which has been output cannot be retrieved—the command **output E** should put **E**'s value directly on to the final answer rather than pass it to the rest of the program embedded in the state.

5.1.4.3. Output can be infinite

The definition **Output = Value*** assumes that the output of programs can be represented by a *finite* string of values. This is incorrect for non-terminating programs like: **x: = 0; while true do (output x; x: = x + 1)** whose output is infinite (namely **0 . 1 . 2 . 3**...).

All the inaccuracies of the last three sections can be corrected if we remove output from the state and change the type of continuations. The required domain equations are:

State	=	**Memory × Input**
Memory	=	**Ide→[Value + {unbound}]**
Input	=	**Value***
Value	=	**Num + Bool**
Cont	=	**State→Ans**
Econt	=	**Value→Cont**
Ans	=	**{error, stop} + [Value × Ans]**

The domain **Ans** of *final answers* is defined recursively (see 3.2.2. and 3.3.4.). A final answer is either **error**, **stop** or a value paired with another answer—'unwinding' this, we see that an answer is either a *finite* string of values ending with **error** or **stop,** or an infinite string of values. Because output is no longer part of the state we must change the semantic clause for **output E** to:

$$\mathbf{C[output\ E]\,c = E[E]\lambda vs\,.\,(v,\,c\,s)}$$

Thus **E** is evaluated to get a value **v** and state **s** and then the final answer is **v** followed by whatever the 'rest of the program' **c** yields when given **s**. This equation models output as a 'system call' to an output device—if the program 'crashes' *after* outputting then the values output will already be in the final answer (e.g. 'printed on the line printer'). For example, if **c = λs . error,** a continuation representing a 'rest of the program' that generates an error for all states, then:

$$\begin{aligned}\mathbf{C[output\ 0]\,c} &= \mathbf{E[0]\lambda v\,s\,.\,(v,\,c\,s)}\\ &= \mathbf{E[0]\lambda v\,s\,.\,(v,\,error)}\\ &= \mathbf{(\lambda v\,s\,.\,(v,\,error))\,0}\\ &= \mathbf{\lambda s\,.\,(0,\,error)}\end{aligned}$$

With the old semantics (with output in the state), outputting is like writing an 'in core' file so that if a 'crash' occurs, all previous output will be lost. For example, recall (C2) in 5.1.3.2.—with that definition of **C[output E]** we get:

$$\begin{aligned}\mathbf{C[output\ 0]\,c} &= \mathbf{E[0]\lambda v(m,i,o)\,.\,c(m,i,v\,.\,o)}\\ &= \mathbf{E[0]\lambda v(m,i,o)\,.\,error}\\ &= \mathbf{E[0]\lambda v\,s\,.\,error}\\ &= \mathbf{(\lambda v\,s\,.\,error)\,0}\\ &= \mathbf{\lambda s\,.\,error}\end{aligned}$$

Using the new continuations with **Ans** we can also express the fact that when a program has finished it should stop. If **C** is a command representing some program to be run then the answer it produces with initial state **s** is just **C[C](λs . stop)s**—the 'rest of the program' represented by the continuation **λs . stop** just outputs **stop** and stops. If **C** were to run on forever **λs . stop** would never be reached.

In general the domain **Ans** of final answers is language-dependent—for some languages (e.g. machine code) it might include the whole state (as we initially had things) or even the sequence of states gone through during the computation. Determining **Ans** is part of the work that has to be done when we write the semantics of a language.

5.2. Locations, stores and environments

In some languages, identifiers are not bound directly to values but instead are bound to things called *variables,* and it is these that possess values. One might think that these variables were formally unnecessary and that (as in TINY) one could just bind each identifier to some value (namely, the value possessed by the corresponding variable). This works fine unless what is called *sharing* (or *aliasing*) is possible.

5.2.1. Sharing

Sometimes distinct identifiers can come to denote the same variable, so that assigning to one of them will have the side effect of changing the value of the other. Such sharing of a single variable by several identifiers (or aliases) may occur as the result of an explicit command or declaration —for example one might have a command **let** $\mathbf{I}_1 == \mathbf{I}_2$ whose evaluation causes $\mathbf{I}_1$ and $\mathbf{I}_2$ to denote the same variable. Sharing can also come about indirectly; for example in PASCAL, if one declares a procedure of the form **procedure P(var x:real; var y:real)**<statement part> and then executes a call **P(z,z),** then inside the body of the procedure (i.e. inside <statement part>) both **x** and **y** will share the variable denoted by **z**.

If sharing is possible then we have no choice but to introduce some model of variables into our semantics. For suppose not; then if $\mathbf{I}_1$ and $\mathbf{I}_2$ share, when we execute the command $\mathbf{I}_1 := \mathbf{1}$ we must ensure in our model that $\mathbf{I}_2$ gets value **1** also. The semantic clause for assignments would thus have to be:

$$\mathbf{C}[\mathbf{I}:=\mathbf{E}]\,\mathbf{c} = \mathbf{E}[\mathbf{E}]\lambda \mathbf{v}(\mathbf{m},\mathbf{i},\mathbf{o})\,.\,\mathbf{c}(\mathbf{m}[\mathbf{v},\mathbf{v},\ldots,\mathbf{v}/\mathbf{I},\mathbf{I}_1,\ldots,\mathbf{I}_n],\mathbf{i},\mathbf{o})$$

where $\mathbf{I}_1,\ldots,\mathbf{I}_n$ are all the identifiers which share with **I**

However to make this precise we have to define what it means for two identifiers to share, and the simplest way of doing this is to say that two identifiers share when they denote the same variable.

5.2.2. Variables and locations

The word "variable" has a number of misleading connotations, so in connection with formal semantics the less loaded term "location" is often used instead. To model locations (i.e. variables) we introduce a new primitive domain, **Loc**, typical members of which are $\mathbf{l}$, $\mathbf{l}'$, $\mathbf{l}_1$, $\mathbf{l}_2$, etc. The only structure we shall assume on **Loc** is that locations can be tested for equality with =. When modelling implementations it may be convenient to make **Loc** more concrete; for example to identify it with **Num**—for abstract semantics this is unnecessary.

5.2.3. Stores

To model the association of locations with values we introduce the concept of a *store*. The domain **Store** of stores is defined by

$$\mathbf{Store} = \mathbf{Loc} \rightarrow [\mathbf{Sv} + \{\mathbf{unused}\}]$$

where **Sv** is a language dependent domain of *storable values*—the values that can be held in locations. Exactly what the storable values of a language are is an important question to ask and forms a dimension along which languages can be classified [Strachey 74]. If $\mathbf{s}\varepsilon\mathbf{Store}$ and $\mathbf{l}\varepsilon\mathbf{Loc}$ then if $\mathbf{s\,l} = \mathbf{v}\varepsilon\mathbf{Sv}$ we say $\mathbf{l}$ has (or holds) value $\mathbf{v}$ and if $\mathbf{s\,l} = \mathbf{unused}$ we say $\mathbf{l}$ is unused in $\mathbf{s}$. Certain constructs (for example ALGOL 60 blocks) cause new locations to come into use, and to model these we assume a function $\mathbf{new{:}Store} \rightarrow [\mathbf{Loc} + \{\mathbf{error}\}]$ which has the property that if $\mathbf{isLoc(new\,s)} = \mathbf{true}$ then $\mathbf{s(new\,s)} = \mathbf{unused}$ – i.e. **new s** is an unused location in **s** (**new s** = **error** means that there are no locations available in **s**). There are serious dangers in only *partially* specifying functions as we have just done for **new**. For example, suppose we had assumed $\mathbf{new{:}Store} \rightarrow \mathbf{Loc}$, and that for all **s**, **s(new s) = unused**. Then for any $\mathbf{v}\varepsilon\mathbf{Sv}$, if $\mathbf{s}\varepsilon\mathbf{Store}$ is defined by $\mathbf{s} = \lambda\mathbf{l}\,.\,\mathbf{v}$ then $\mathbf{v} = \mathbf{s(new\,s)} = \mathbf{unused}$! The lesson to learn from this is that one must be *very* careful about *assuming* there exist functions with given properties. In fact the assumptions we made are safe. To see that there do exist **new**'s satisfying them we arbitrarily choose $\mathbf{l}_1, \mathbf{l}_2, \ldots, \mathbf{l}_n \varepsilon \mathbf{Loc}$ and then *define* **new** by:

$$\begin{aligned}\mathbf{new} = \lambda\mathbf{s}\,.\,\mathbf{s\,l}_1 &= \mathbf{unused} \rightarrow \mathbf{l}_1,\\ \mathbf{s\,l}_2 &= \mathbf{unused} \rightarrow \mathbf{l}_2,\\ &\vdots\\ \mathbf{s\,l}_n &= \mathbf{unused} \rightarrow \mathbf{l}_n, \mathbf{error}\end{aligned}$$

This models finite stores with locations $\mathbf{l}_1$, $\mathbf{l}_2$, ..., $\mathbf{l}_n$, where **new s** is the first unused $\mathbf{l}_i$ (or **error** if all the $\mathbf{l}_i$'s are in use). Clearly for *this particular* **new,** if **isLoc(new s) = true** then **s(new s) = unused**. When modelling implementations it is necessary to specify details of storage allocation and so particular **new**'s must be defined; however for our purposes this is unnecessary. Finally note that we shall use **s**, $\mathbf{s}_1$, $\mathbf{s}_2$, etc., to range over **store** and $\mathbf{v}_1,\ldots,\mathbf{v}_n/\mathbf{l}_1,\ldots,\mathbf{l}_n$ to denote the 'little' store defined by:

$$\begin{aligned}\mathbf{v}_1,\ldots,\mathbf{v}_n/\mathbf{l}_1,\ldots,\mathbf{l}_n = \lambda\mathbf{l}\,.\,\mathbf{l} &= \mathbf{l}_1 \rightarrow \mathbf{v}_1,\\ \mathbf{l} &= \mathbf{l}_2 \rightarrow \mathbf{v}_2,\\ &\vdots\\ \mathbf{l} &= \mathbf{l}_n \rightarrow \mathbf{v}_n,\ \mathbf{unused}\end{aligned}$$

Thus in $\mathbf{v}_1,\ldots,\mathbf{v}_n/\mathbf{l}_1,\ldots,\mathbf{l}_n$ the only locations in use are $\mathbf{l}_1,\ldots,\mathbf{l}_n$ and these hold $\mathbf{v}_1,\ldots,\mathbf{v}_n$ respectively.

5.2.4. Environments

To model the binding of identifiers we use the concept of an *environment*. The domain **Env** of environments is defined by

$$\mathbf{Env} = \mathbf{Ide} \rightarrow [\mathbf{Dv} + \{\mathbf{unbound}\}]$$

where **Dv** is the language-dependent domain of *denotable values.* If the only thing identifiers can be bound to is locations then **Dv** = **Loc**; however in most languages identifiers can denote other things besides locations—for example, constants (e.g. numbers), arrays, records, procedures, etc. Exactly what the denotable values are is an important question to ask about a language and, like the storable values, forms a dimension for classification. We shall use **r**, **r**′, $\mathbf{r}_1$, $\mathbf{r}_2$, etc., to range over **Env,** and also the following two notations:

(i) If $\mathbf{d}_1,\ldots,\mathbf{d}_n \varepsilon \mathbf{Dv}$ and $\mathbf{I}_1,\ldots,\mathbf{I}_n \varepsilon \mathbf{Ide}$ then $\mathbf{d}_1,\ldots,\mathbf{d}_n/\mathbf{I}_1,\ldots,\mathbf{I}_n$ is the 'little' environment defined by

$$\begin{aligned}\mathbf{d}_1,\ldots,\mathbf{d}_n/\mathbf{I}_1,\ldots,\mathbf{I}_n = \lambda\mathbf{I}\,.\,\mathbf{I} &= \mathbf{I}_1 \rightarrow \mathbf{d}_1,\\ &\vdots\\ \mathbf{I} &= \mathbf{I}_n \rightarrow \mathbf{d}_n,\ \mathbf{unbound}\end{aligned}$$

(ii) If $\mathbf{r}_1, \mathbf{r}_2 \varepsilon \mathbf{Env}$ then $\mathbf{r}_1[\mathbf{r}_2] \varepsilon \mathbf{Env}$ is defined by:

$$\mathbf{r}_1[\mathbf{r}_2] = \lambda \mathbf{I} \,.\, \mathbf{r}_2\mathbf{I} = \mathbf{unbound} \rightarrow \mathbf{r}_1\mathbf{I}, \mathbf{r}_2\mathbf{I}$$

If we put (i) and (ii) together we get

$$\begin{aligned} \mathbf{r}[\mathbf{d}_1,\ldots,\mathbf{d}_n/\mathbf{I}_1,\ldots,\mathbf{I}_n] = \lambda \mathbf{I} \,.\, \mathbf{I} &= \mathbf{I}_1 \rightarrow \mathbf{d}_1, \\ &\vdots \\ \mathbf{I} &= \mathbf{I}_n \rightarrow \mathbf{d}_n, \mathbf{r}\,\mathbf{I} \end{aligned}$$

which is consistent with the notation described in 3.4.7.

5.3. Standard domains of values

In TINY we had just one domain of values, namely **Value**. In general one needs to distinguish several value domains, among the most important of which are:

(i) *Storable* values **Sv**—the values which can be stored in locations in the store. We use $\mathbf{v}$, $\mathbf{v}'$, $\mathbf{v}_1$, $\mathbf{v}_2$, etc., to range over **Sv**.

(ii) *Denotable* values **Dv**—the values which can be bound to (or "denoted by") identifiers in the environment. We use $\mathbf{d}$, $\mathbf{d}'$, $\mathbf{d}_1$, $\mathbf{d}_2$ etc. to range over **Dv**.

(iii) *Expressible* values **Ev**—the values expressions can produce as results. We use $\mathbf{e}$, $\mathbf{e}'$, $\mathbf{e}_1$, $\mathbf{e}_2$, etc., to range over **Ev**.

Although these domains usually intersect they are conceptually distinct and are not normally the same. For example, in PASCAL, constants such as numbers and truth values are denotable, but in ALGOL 60 they are not. In PASCAL, locations are storable, but in ALGOL 60 they are not. Other domains of values besides **Sv**, **Dv** and **Ev** may also be needed for particular languages. For example, one may need to explicitly distinguish and define the 'outputable values' or the values that can be passed to procedures. Another general purpose value domain which we discuss later (in 5.8.) is **Rv**, the domain of *R-values*—this is the domain of 'dereferenced' expression values (called "R-values" because they are extracted on the right of assignments).

5.4. Blocks, declarations and scope

In languages like ALGOL 60 and PASCAL, commands change the

contents of locations but not the binding of identifiers to locations. For example, in the ALGOL 60 program:

```
begin integer x;
                :
             x:=1;
                :
             x:=2;
                :
end
```

throughout the body of the block (the text between **begin** and **end**) **x** denotes a *fixed* location, ι say, in the environment; but the contents of ι changes with each assignment to **x**. The only way bindings in the environment can be changed is with *declarations*. For example in

```
begin integer x;
      integer y;
             :
      begin   integer x;
                      :
      end
         :
end
```

the **x** in the inner and outer blocks denote different locations. Since **y** is not declared in the inner block, it denotes the same location in this as it does in the outer block. Each declaration 'holds' throughout a certain part of the program. In ALGOL 60, declarations hold throughout the body of the block in which they are introduced unless they are *overwritten* by a declaration in an inner block. In PASCAL, declarations hold throughout the procedure body at whose head they occur unless they are overwritten by a with-statement (see 9.) within this procedure body. In the example above (which is based on ALGOL 60), the outer declaration of **x** holds throughout the parts of the outer block not included in the inner one. The declaration of **y** holds throughout the whole outer block. If **x** (like **y**) were not declared in the inner block then its outer declaration would hold there also.

The parts of a program where a declaration holds are called its *scope*.

The example above illustrates *holes* in scope: the inner block is a hole in the scope of the outer declaration of **x** but not of **y**. The scope of an identifier with respect to a declaration is the scope of the declaration. If this declaration is unique (or defined by the context) then we can unambiguously talk about the scope of the identifier. Thus "the scope of **y**" makes sense in the above example, but not "the scope of **x**"—the latter phrase is ambiguous between the scopes of the inner and outer declarations of **x**.

In standard semantics:

(i) Commands change the store but not the environment.
(ii) Declarations change the environment (and possibly also the store).

Thus environments only change at 'scope boundaries'. Declarations may change the store as well as the environment since—for example, in the case of variable declarations—they may 'allocate' new storage (i.e. put new locations into use). In the language SMALL, described below in 6., there are variable declarations of the form **var I = E** which have the effect that:

(i) A new location, **ɩ** say, is obtained.
(ii) **E**'s value is stored in **ɩ**.
(iii) **ɩ** is bound to **I** in the environment.

(ii) changes the store and (iii) the environment.

In general the declarations of a language form a syntactic category modelled by a syntactic domain **Dec**. We shall use **D** to range over **Dec** and $\mathbf{D}$ for the associated semantic function (see 5.6.). In SMALL, **Dec** will be defined by:

$$\mathbf{D} ::= \mathbf{const\ I = E} \mid \mathbf{var\ I = E} \mid \mathbf{proc\ I(I_1);C} \mid \mathbf{fun\ I(I_1);E} \mid \mathbf{D_1;D_2}$$

var I = E is as just described; **const I = E** binds **E**'s value directly to **I** in the environment (and so does not change the store); **proc I(I_1);C** declares a *procedure* named **I** with *formal parameter* $\mathbf{I_1}$ and *body* **C** (see 5.9.1. for details); **fun I(I_1);E** declares a *function* named **I** with formal parameter $\mathbf{I_1}$ and body **E** (see 5.9.2.); and finally, $\mathbf{D_1;D_2}$ is a *compound declaration* whose effects are those of $\mathbf{D_1}$ followed by those of $\mathbf{D_2}$.

In the semantics (see 5.5.3. and 5.6.) each declaration generates a 'little' environment containing the bindings it specifies. For example,

const I = **E** generates **e**/**I** where **e** is **E**'s value, whereas **var I** = **E** generates **ι**/**I** where **ι** is a new location updated with **E**'s value. This little environment is then passed, together with a possibly changed store, to the rest of the program following the declaration.

5.5. Standard domains of continuations

In standard semantics three main kinds of continuation are used.

5.5.1. Command continuations

Since commands pass a store to the rest of the program following them we define **Cc**—the domain of *command continuations*—by

$$\mathbf{Cc} = \mathbf{Store} \to \mathbf{Ans}$$

where **Ans** is the domain of *final answers.* The exact structure of **Ans** is language-dependent; all we shall assume is that it contains an error element **error**. We shall use $\mathbf{c}$, $\mathbf{c}'$, $\mathbf{c}_1$, $\mathbf{c}_2$, etc., to range over **Cc**.

5.5.2. Expression continuations

Since expressions pass their values, together with a possibly changed store, to the rest of the program following them, we define **Ec**—the domain of *expression continuations*—by:

$$\mathbf{Ec} = \mathbf{Ev} \to \mathbf{Store} \to \mathbf{Ans}$$

or more neatly:

$$\mathbf{Ec} = \mathbf{Ev} \to \mathbf{Cc}$$

We use $\mathbf{k}$, $\mathbf{k}'$, $\mathbf{k}_1$, $\mathbf{k}_2$, etc., to range over **Ec**.

5.5.3. Declaration continuations

Since declarations pass an environment, together with a possibly changed store, to the rest of the program following them, we define **Dc**—the domain of *declaration continuations*—by:

$$\mathbf{Dc} = \mathbf{Env} \to \mathbf{Store} \to \mathbf{Ans}$$

or more neatly:

$$\mathbf{Dc} = \mathbf{Env} \rightarrow \mathbf{Cc}$$

We use $\mathbf{u}$, $\mathbf{u}'$, $\mathbf{u}_1$, $\mathbf{u}_2$, etc., to range over **Dc**.

5.6. Standard semantic functions

In a standard semantics we use semantic functions with the following types:

$$\mathbf{E}: \mathbf{Exp} \rightarrow \mathbf{Env} \rightarrow \mathbf{Ec} \rightarrow \mathbf{Store} \rightarrow \mathbf{Ans}$$
$$\mathbf{C}: \mathbf{Com} \rightarrow \mathbf{Env} \rightarrow \mathbf{Cc} \rightarrow \mathbf{Store} \rightarrow \mathbf{Ans}$$
$$\mathbf{D}: \mathbf{Dec} \rightarrow \mathbf{Env} \rightarrow \mathbf{Dc} \rightarrow \mathbf{Store} \rightarrow \mathbf{Ans}$$

When no errors, jumps, etc., occur, the intuitive meanings of these functions are:

$\mathbf{E[E]\,r\,k\,s} = \mathbf{k\,e\,s'}$ where **e** is **E**'s value in environment **r** and store **s**, and **s**′ is the store after **E**'s evaluation.

$\mathbf{C[C]\,r\,c\,s} = \mathbf{c\,s'}$ where **s**′ is the store resulting from executing **C** in environment **r** and store **s**.

$\mathbf{D[D]\,r\,u\,s} = \mathbf{u\,r'\,s'}$ where **r**′ is the environment consisting of the 'bindings' specified in **D** (when evaluated with respect to **r** and **s**), and **s**′ the store resulting from **D**'s evaluation.

Thus each semantic function passes the appropriate intermediate results to its continuation. Examples of typical semantic clauses for SMALL are

(E1) $\mathbf{E[0]\,r\,k\,s} = \mathbf{k\,0\,s}$

0's value **0** is passed, together with an unchanged store, to **k**.

(C7) $\mathbf{C[C_1;C_2]\,r\,c\,s} = \mathbf{C[C_1]\,r\,(\lambda s'\,.\,C[C_2]\,r\,c\,s')\,s}$

$\mathbf{C}_1$ is executed in environment **r** and store **s** to get a store **s**′ which is passed to the continuation $\lambda\mathbf{s}'\,.\,\mathbf{C[C_2]\,r\,c\,s'}$, which executes $\mathbf{C}_2$ in the same environment but in store **s**′, and then finally sends the resulting store on to **c**. Notice that since commands don't change the environment, **r** is passed to both $\mathbf{C}_1$ and $\mathbf{C}_2$. Note also that the semantic clause can be simplified to

$$\mathbf{C}[\![C_1;C_2]\!]\,r\,c = \mathbf{C}[\![C_1]\!]\,r\,(\mathbf{C}[\![C_2]\!]\,r\,c)$$ (see 3.4.10.)

or $$\mathbf{C}[\![C_1;C_2]\!]\,r\,c = \mathbf{C}[\![C_1]\!]\,r;\mathbf{C}[\![C_2]\!]\,r\,c$$ (see 3.4.3. (iii))

or even $$\mathbf{C}[\![C_1;C_2]\!]\,r = \mathbf{C}[\![C_1]\!]\,r \circ \mathbf{C}[\![C_2]\!]\,r$$ (see 3.4.12.1.).

(D1) $\mathbf{D}[\![\mathbf{const}\ I = E]\!]\,r\,u\,s = \mathbf{E}[\![E]\!]\,r\,(\lambda e s'.\,u(e/I)s')\,s$

Here **E**'s value **e** is bound to **I** to form the little environment **e/I** which is passed on to **u** together with the store **s**′ resulting from **E**'s evaluation. The clause can be simplified to:

$$\mathbf{D}[\![\mathbf{const}\ I = E]\!]\,r\,u = \mathbf{E}[\![E]\!]\,r\,\lambda e.\,u(e/I)$$

(N.B. This clause, although right in spirit, has a minor error—the value of **E** needs to be 'dereferenced' before being bound to **I**. See 5.8 for a discussion and 6.2.3.4. for the correct equation).

The rest of the semantic clauses for SMALL are explained in the next chapter (specifically 6.2.3.).

5.7. Continuation transforming functions

In this section we describe some functions for transforming continuations. These functions *intuitively* transform values and stores to new values and stores, but are defined over continuations to make them convenient for use in continuation semantics. The general idea is as follows: suppose **f:Ev→Store→[[Ev × Store] + {error}]**. Then instead of using **f** we shall use **f′:Ec→Ec**, defined by:

$$f'\,k = \lambda e s.\,(f\,e\,s = (e',s')) \rightarrow k\,e'\,s',\ \mathbf{error}$$
$$= f \star k \quad \text{(using } \star \text{ as defined in 3.4.12.2.)}$$

Thus **f**′ takes a continuation **k** and produces another continuation which first does **f** and then passes the results to **k**. The relationship between **f** and **f**′ can be factored out into a function **mkconfun**, defined so that **f**′ = **mkconfun f**. The appropriate definition is simply:

$$\mathbf{mkconfun} = \lambda f k.\,f \star k$$

The use of these continuation transformers is as follows: frequently we want to evaluate an expression, **E**, and then transform the resulting values by a sequence of functions, $f_1,\ldots,f_n$, and then pass the result of these transformations to the 'rest of the program', **k**. Now if

$\mathbf{f_1', \ldots, f_n': Ec \rightarrow Ec}$ are the continuation transformations corresponding to $\mathbf{f_1, \ldots, f_n}$(i.e. $\mathbf{f_i'}$ = **mkconfun** $\mathbf{f_i}$) then the desired effect is modelled by:

$$\mathbf{E[E]\ r\ (f_1'(f_2' \ldots (f_n'\ k) \ldots))}$$

or using ";" (see 3.4.3.):

$$\mathbf{E[E]\ r; f_1'; \ldots; f_n'; k}$$

To see that this works we simply note that

$$\mathbf{f_1'(f_2' \ldots (f_n'\ k) \ldots) = f_1 \star f_2 \star \ldots \star f_n \star k}$$

Summing up, an expression like $\mathbf{E[E]\ r; f_1'; \ldots; f_n'; k}$ should be 'read' as "evaluate **E**, do $\mathbf{f_1', \ldots, f_n'}$ and then pass the results to **k**".

In what follows we define the continuation transformations (e.g. $\mathbf{f_1'}$) directly since the non-continuation ones (e.g. $\mathbf{f_1}$) will not be of use to us. If we were going to use direct semantics then it would be the non-continuation transformations that we would need. For example, compare **checkNum** and **checkBool** which we used in the direct semantics of TINY (see 4.2.2.) with **Num?** and **Bool?** which are what we shall use with continuations (see 5.7.6.).

5.7.1. cont:Ec→Ec

Informal description

cont k e s checks that **e** is a location and if so, looks up its contents in **s** and passes the result, together with **s**, to **k**. If **e** is not a location, or if it is but is unused in **s**, then **cont k e s = error**.

Formal description

cont = λk e s . isLoc e→(s e = unused→error, k(s e)s), error

5.7.2. update:Loc→Cc→Ec

Informal description

update ι c e s stores **e** at location **ι** in **s** and passes the resulting store to **c**. If **e** is not a storable value then **update ι c e s = error**.

Formal description

$$\textbf{update} = \lambda\iota\,\textbf{c}\,\textbf{e}\,\textbf{s}\,.\,\textbf{isSv}\;\textbf{e}\rightarrow\textbf{c}(\textbf{s}[\textbf{e}/\iota]),\ \textbf{error}$$

5.7.3. ref:Ec→Ec

Informal description

ref k e s gets an unused location from **s**, updates it with **e** and then passes it, and the updated store, to **k**. If **s** has no unused locations available then **ref k e s** = **error**.

Formal description

$$\textbf{ref} = \lambda\textbf{k}\,\textbf{e}\,\textbf{s}\,.\,\textbf{new}\,\textbf{s} = \textbf{error}\rightarrow\textbf{error},\ \textbf{update}\,(\textbf{new}\,\textbf{s})(\textbf{k}(\textbf{new}\,\textbf{s}))\textbf{e}\,\textbf{s}$$

5.7.4. deref:Ec→Ec

Informal description

deref k e s tests whether **e** is a location and if so, passes its contents in **s**, together with **s**, to **k**. If **e** is not a location, then **e** and **s** are passed to **k**.

Formal description

$$\textbf{deref} = \lambda\textbf{k}\,\textbf{e}\,\textbf{s}\,.\,\textbf{isLoc}\;\textbf{e}\rightarrow\textbf{cont}\;\textbf{k}\,\textbf{e}\,\textbf{s},\ \textbf{k}\,\textbf{e}\,\textbf{s}$$

5.7.5. err:Cc

Informal description

err is the error continuation.

Formal description

$$\textbf{err} = \lambda\textbf{s}\,.\,\textbf{error}$$

5.7.6. Domain checks: D?:Ec→Ec

Informal description

For each summand **D** of **Ev** we define a function **D?** which checks whether an element is in **D** and produces an error if not. **D? k e s** passes **e** and **s** to **k** if **e** is in **D**, and is **error** otherwise.

Formal description

$$\mathbf{D?} = \lambda \mathbf{k}\,\mathbf{e}\,.\,\mathbf{isD}\ \mathbf{e} \rightarrow \mathbf{k}\ \mathbf{e},\ \mathbf{err}$$

Examples

$$\begin{aligned} \text{If } \mathbf{Ev} &= \mathbf{Num} + \mathbf{Bool} + \ldots \text{ then} \\ \mathbf{Num?} &= \lambda \mathbf{k}\,\mathbf{e}\,.\,\mathbf{isNum}\ \mathbf{e} \rightarrow \mathbf{k}\ \mathbf{e},\ \mathbf{err} \\ \mathbf{Bool?} &= \lambda \mathbf{k}\,\mathbf{e}\,.\,\mathbf{isBool}\ \mathbf{e} \rightarrow \mathbf{k}\ \mathbf{e},\ \mathbf{err} \end{aligned}$$

5.8. Assignment and L and R values

The meaning of an assignment **I** := **E** in TINY is the function which takes a state and then updates the memory component at **I** with **E**'s value. In standard semantics—where instead of states we have environments and stores—**E** is evaluated and its value stored in the location, **ι** say, denoted by **I** in the environment (if **I** does not denote a location then an error results). The assignment only changes the contents of **ι** in the store; the binding of **I** to **ι** in the environment is unaffected.

Suppose $\mathbf{I}_1$ and $\mathbf{I}_2$ denote locations $\mathbf{\iota}_1$ and $\mathbf{\iota}_2$ in the environment; then what is the effect of $\mathbf{I}_1 := \mathbf{I}_2$? There are two obvious possibilities:

(i) Location $\mathbf{\iota}_2$ is stored in location $\mathbf{\iota}_1$.
(ii) The *contents* of location $\mathbf{\iota}_2$ is stored in location $\mathbf{\iota}_1$.

In both ALGOL 60 and PASCAL (ii) describes what happens (in PASCAL the effect of (i) can be obtained using pointers—see 9.1.).

Thus in standard semantics we shall assume that expressions occurring on the *right* of assignments have their values *dereferenced*—i.e. have their value looked up in the store if they are locations.

On the *left* of assignments, however, we need a location, not its contents, since it is a location we update. The dereferencing that is necessary on the right hand side can be done with the function **deref** defined in 5.7.4. If **k** is a continuation expecting a dereferenced value (e.g. the 'rest of the program' following an expression on the right of an assignment) then **deref k** is a continuation which when sent an undereferenced value will first dereference it and then send the result to **k**. The standard semantics of **I** := **E** is thus:

$$
\begin{aligned}
&\mathbf{C[I := E]\ r\ c\ s} = \\
&\quad \mathbf{E[I]\ r\ k_1\ s} \\
&\quad \mathbf{where\ k_1 = \lambda e_1\ s_1\ .\ isLoc\ e_1 \rightarrow E[E]\ r\ k_2\ s_1,\ error} \\
&\qquad \mathbf{where\ k_2 = \lambda e_2\ s_2\ .\ deref\ k_3\ e_2\ s_2} \\
&\qquad\quad \mathbf{where\ k_3 = \lambda e_3\ s_3\ .\ update\ e_1\ c\ e_3\ s_3}
\end{aligned}
$$

We evaluate **I** and pass the results to $\mathbf{k_1}$. $\mathbf{k_1}$ takes the results, $\mathbf{e_1}$ and $\mathbf{s_1}$, of **I**'s evaluation, checks that $\mathbf{e_1}$ is a location, and then evaluates **E** and passes the results to $\mathbf{k_2}$. $\mathbf{k_2}$ takes the results, $\mathbf{e_2}$ and $\mathbf{s_2}$, of **E**, dereferences $\mathbf{e_2}$, and passes the results to $\mathbf{k_3}$. $\mathbf{k_3}$ takes the results, $\mathbf{e_3}$ and $\mathbf{s_3}$, of dereferencing $\mathbf{e_2}$, updates the location $\mathbf{e_1}$ with contents $\mathbf{e_3}$, and then passes the resulting store to **c**. This semantic clause can be simplified. First notice that:

$$\mathbf{k_3 = update\ e_1\ c}$$

$$
\begin{aligned}
\text{hence}\quad \mathbf{k_2} &= \mathbf{deref\ k_3} \\
&= \mathbf{deref;update\ e_1;c}
\end{aligned}
$$

$$
\begin{aligned}
\text{hence}\quad \mathbf{k_1} &= \mathbf{\lambda e_1\ .\ isLoc\ e_1 \rightarrow E[E]\ r;deref;update\ e_1;c,\ err} \\
&= \mathbf{\lambda e_1\ .\ Loc?(\lambda\iota\ .\ E[E]\ r;deref;update\ \iota;c)e_1} \\
&= \mathbf{Loc?\ \lambda\iota\ .\ E[E]\ r;deref;update\ \iota;c}
\end{aligned}
$$

and thus:

$$\mathbf{C[I := E]\ r\ c = E[I]\ r;Loc?\ \lambda\iota\ .\ E[E]\ r;deref;update\ \iota;c}$$

5.8.1. L and R values

To distinguish the different values extracted from expressions during assignments the following terminology is often used:

(i) The value of an expression needed on the *left* of an assignment is the expression's *L-value*. This value is a location and is obtained by the semantic function **E** without any dereferencing.

(ii) The value of an expression needed on the right of an assignment is the expression's *R-value.* This value is (normally) obtained by dereferencing the value obtained with **E**.

There are often other contexts besides the right hand sides of assignments in which we need to dereference expression values. For example, in

output E, if **E**'s value is a location (e.g. **E** = **I**), then we should output its contents. Rather than continually write **E[E] r;deref** it is traditional to define a new semantic function **R** for obtaining R-values:

R:Exp→Env→Ec→Cc

defined by: **R[E] r k = E[E] r (deref k)**

A function **L:Exp→Env→Ec→Cc** defined by **L[E] r k = E[E] r (Loc? k)** which obtains L-values is also sometimes used. Using **L** and **R**, the semantic clause for assignments becomes simply:

$$\mathbf{C[I := E]\,r\,c = L[I]\,r\,\lambda\iota\,.\,R[E]\,r;update\,\iota;c}$$

In some languages, only a subset of the expressible values are allowed as the contents of locations. For example, in PASCAL procedures are expressible but cannot be assigned to variables. The storable subset of **Ev** is the domain **Rv** of R-values, and it is convenient to make the semantic function **R** check that it only produces R-values. Thus, in this case, we define:

$$\mathbf{R[E]\,r\,k = E[E]\,r;deref;Rv?;k}$$

5.9. Procedures and functions

In this section we outline the standard semantics of declarations and calls of procedures and functions. Note that by "functions" we mean the programming concept of a function—see the discussion at the beginning of 3.4.

5.9.1. Procedures

A procedure, declared by **proc** $\mathbf{I(I_1);C}$, say, has *name* **I**, *formal parameter* $\mathbf{I_1}$ and *body* **C**. Within the scope of its declaration it can be *called*, for example, by a command of the form **I(E)**. The effect of this is to execute the body **C** in an environment identical to the environment in which the procedure was declared, except that the formal parameter $\mathbf{I_1}$ denotes **E**'s value. The evaluation of procedure bodies in an environment derived from the *declaration time* environment is called *static binding*. Other kinds of binding, using other environments, are possible (for example *dynamic binding*—found in LISP and POP-2—uses the *call time* environment). The semantics and merits of different kinds of binding are discussed in detail in 8.3.; for the time being we stick to static binding since it is the one used in ALGOL 60 and PASCAL. The expression **E**, in a call **I(E)**, is called the *actual parameter*—thus when a procedure is called, the actual parameter value is bound to the formal parameter. The semantics of a procedure declaration is to bind some 'procedure value' to the procedure name in the environment; thus:

$$\mathbf{D[proc\ I(I_1);C]\ r\ u = u(p/I)}$$

where **p** is a procedure value modelling a procedure with formal parameter $\mathbf{I_1}$ and body **C**.

Procedure values are members of the domain **Proc** defined by:

$$\mathbf{Proc = Cc \to Ev \to Store \to Ans}$$

We use **p**, **p'**, $\mathbf{p_1}$, $\mathbf{p_2}$, etc., to range over **Proc**. The definition of **Proc** can be simplified to:

$$\mathbf{Proc = Cc \to Ec}$$

The intuitive idea is that if $\mathbf{p \varepsilon Proc}$ then:

$\mathbf{p\,c\,e\,s = c\,s'}$ where **s'** is the store resulting from executing **p**'s body with actual parameter **e** and store **s**.

The continuation **c** passed to procedure values is analogous to the 'return address' in an implementation—it enables the procedure to return to the rest of the program following its call when execution of its body has finished. The complete semantic clause for procedure declarations can now be given:

$$\mathbf{D[proc\ I(I_1);C]\ r\ u = u(p/I)}$$
$$\mathbf{where\ p = \lambda c\,e\,.\,C[C]\,r[e/I_1]\,c}$$

Notice that the environment $\mathbf{r[e/I_1]}$ in which the body **C** is evaluated is derived from the declaration time environment **r**—i.e. we have static binding. Notice also that for this equation to make sense, **p** must be a denotable value—i.e. **Dv = ... + Proc + ...**

The semantics of a procedure call is given by:

$$\mathcal{C}[\![\mathbf{I(E)}]\!]\,\mathbf{r\,c\,s} = $$
$$\mathcal{E}[\![\mathbf{I}]\!]\,\mathbf{r}(\lambda \mathbf{e}_1\,\mathbf{s}_1\,.\ \mathbf{isProc}\ \mathbf{e}_1 \rightarrow \mathcal{E}[\![\mathbf{E}]\!]\,\mathbf{r}(\lambda \mathbf{e}_2\,\mathbf{s}_2\,.\ \mathbf{e}_1\,\mathbf{c}\,\mathbf{e}_2\,\mathbf{s}_2)\mathbf{s}_1,\ \mathbf{error})\mathbf{s}$$

We evaluate **I** to get $\mathbf{e}_1$ and $\mathbf{s}_1$, and check that $\mathbf{e}_1$ is a procedure value. If it is not, then an error occurs. If it is, we evaluate **E** in $\mathbf{s}_1$ to get **e** and $\mathbf{s}_2$, and then apply $\mathbf{e}_1$ to 'return address' **c**, actual parameter value $\mathbf{e}_2$ and store $\mathbf{s}_2$. This equation can be written more compactly as

$$\mathcal{C}[\![\mathbf{I(E)}]\!]\,\mathbf{r\,c} = \mathcal{E}[\![\mathbf{I}]\!]\,\mathbf{r};\mathbf{Proc?}\,\lambda \mathbf{p}\,.\,\mathcal{E}[\![\mathbf{E}]\!]\,\mathbf{r};\mathbf{p\,c}$$

which can be 'read' as: "evaluate **I**, check that the result is in **Proc;** if so, call the result **p**, evaluate **E**, and pass its value to **p c**".

5.9.2. Functions

In many languages one can declare 'functions' which, when called, return a value as a result of the call. For example, if **fact** is such a function, then **fact(n)** is an expression, and things like **output fact(n)** make sense. Note that these 'functions' must be carefully distinguished from the mathematical functions they denote. In both ALGOL 60 and PASCAL the result of a function is the last value assigned to the function name in its body. For example, in PASCAL, a function to square an integer **n** would be declared thus:

function square (n:integer):integer; begin square: = n × n end

Since function calls are expressions, the continuation passed to a function value must be an expression continuation. Thus we define the domain **Fun** of function values by:

$$\mathbf{Fun} = \mathbf{Ec} \rightarrow \mathbf{Ec}$$

We use **f**, **f′**, $\mathbf{f}_1$, $\mathbf{f}_2$, etc., to range over **Fun**. The semantics of function calls is

$$\mathcal{E}[\![\mathbf{I(E)}]\!]\,\mathbf{r\,k} = \mathcal{E}[\![\mathbf{I}]\!]\,\mathbf{r};\mathbf{Fun?}\,\lambda \mathbf{f}\,.\,\mathcal{E}[\![\mathbf{E}]\!]\,\mathbf{r};\mathbf{f\,k}$$

which can be understood by analogy with the clause for procedure calls which it closely resembles. Note that for this to make sense, **f**'s must be denotable.

In SMALL (see next chapter), function declarations are of the form **fun** $\mathbf{I(I_1);E}$. Thus the body of a function is an *expression* which, when evaluated, yields the value to be returned. This way of yielding values is much cleaner than assigning to the function's name; we discuss some of the problems of that in 8.2.1. The semantic clause for function declarations is similar to the one for procedures:

$$\mathcal{D}[\![\mathbf{fun}\,\mathbf{I}(\mathbf{I}_1);\mathbf{E}]\!]\,\mathbf{r}\,\mathbf{u} = \mathbf{u}(\mathbf{f}/\mathbf{I}) \quad \text{where } \mathbf{f} = \lambda \mathbf{k}\,\mathbf{e}\,.\,\mathcal{E}[\![\mathbf{E}]\!]\,\mathbf{r}[\mathbf{e}/\mathbf{I}_1]\,\mathbf{k}$$

5.9.3. Summary

Domains: **Proc** = **Cc→Ec**—procedure values **p**
Fun = **Ec→Ec**—function values **f**

Clauses for declarations:

$$\mathcal{D}[\![\mathbf{proc}\ \mathbf{I}(\mathbf{I}_1);\mathbf{C}]\!]\,\mathbf{r}\,\mathbf{u} = \mathbf{u}((\lambda \mathbf{c}\,\mathbf{e}\,.\,\mathcal{C}[\![\mathbf{C}]\!]\,\mathbf{r}[\mathbf{e}/\mathbf{I}_1]\,\mathbf{c})/\mathbf{I})$$
$$\mathcal{D}[\![\mathbf{fun}\ \mathbf{I}(\mathbf{I}_1);\mathbf{E}]\!]\,\mathbf{r}\,\mathbf{u} = \mathbf{u}((\lambda \mathbf{k}\,\mathbf{e}\,.\,\mathcal{E}[\![\mathbf{E}]\!]\,\mathbf{r}[\mathbf{e}/\mathbf{I}_1]\,\mathbf{k})/\mathbf{I})$$

Clauses for calls:

$$\mathcal{C}[\![\mathbf{I}(\mathbf{E})]\!]\,\mathbf{r}\,\mathbf{c} = \mathcal{E}[\![\mathbf{I}]\!]\,\mathbf{r};\mathbf{Proc}?\,\lambda \mathbf{p}\,.\,\mathcal{E}[\![\mathbf{E}]\!]\,\mathbf{r};\mathbf{p}\,\mathbf{c}$$
$$\mathcal{E}[\![\mathbf{I}(\mathbf{E})]\!]\,\mathbf{r}\,\mathbf{k} = \mathcal{E}[\![\mathbf{I}]\!]\,\mathbf{r};\mathbf{Fun}?\,\lambda \mathbf{f}\,.\,\mathcal{E}[\![\mathbf{E}]\!]\,\mathbf{r};\mathbf{f}\,\mathbf{k}$$

5.10. Non-standard semantics and concurrency

Standard semantics is based on the idea that the meaning of a construct is its effect on the final answers of programs in which it occurs. This implies, for example, that **x := 2** and **x := 1;x := x+1** have the same meaning. For most purposes this is exactly what we want, but not always. Consider a language containing a construct **cobegin** $\mathbf{C}_1,\mathbf{C}_2$ **coend** whose meaning is that $\mathbf{C}_1$ and $\mathbf{C}_2$ are executed *concurrently* until they both terminate. In such a language, **x : = 2** and **x : = 1;x : = x + 1** must have different denotations because, for example, **cobegin x : = 2, x : = 2 coend** can have different effects from **cobegin x : = 2, x : = 1;x : = x + 1 coend**. In the second case the **x : = 2** might be done after the **x : = 1** but before the **x : = x + 1**, resulting in **x** denoting **3**. The only result of **cobegin x : = 2, x : = 2 coend** is for **x** to denote **2**. If we had $\mathcal{C}[\![\mathbf{x := 2}]\!] = \mathcal{C}[\![\mathbf{x := 1;x := x + 1}]\!]$ then, since the denotation of a construct must depend only on the denotations of its immediate constituents, no matter how we defined **C[cobegin** C_1, C_2 **coend]** we would have:

C[cobegin x := 2, x := 1;x := x + 1 **coend]**
= ...C[x := 2]...C[x := 1;x := x + 1]...
= ...C[x := 2]...C[x := 2]...
= **C[cobegin** x := 2, x := 2 **coend]**

To enable a semantics of **cobegin** C_1, C_2 **coend** to be given, each command must denote some sort of 'process' in which the 'interleavable operations' are modelled (see [Milner] for example); in such cases standard semantics is not appropriate. Non-standard semantics are also useful for modelling implementations; see [Milne and Strachey].

6. A second example: the Language SMALL

The language SMALL described in this chapter has two roles:

(i) To illustrate the main ideas of standard semantics.
(ii) To provide a 'kernel language' which we shall extend as we discuss the semantics of various constructs in later chapters.

6.1. Syntax of SMALL

6.1.1. Syntactic domains

The *primitive* syntactic domains of SMALL are:

Ide	The domain of identifiers **I**
Bas	The domain of basic constants **B**
Opr	The domain of binary operators **O**

We do not further specify these primitive domains. **Bas** could, for example, be {**0, 1, 2, ...**} and **Opr** could be $\{+, -, \times, /, <, >, \ldots\}$.

The *compound* syntactic domains of SMALL are:

Pro	The domain of programs **P**
Exp	The domain of expressions **E**
Com	The domain of commands **C**
Dec	The domain of declarations **D**

These domains are defined by the following syntactic clauses:

6.1.2. Syntactic clauses

$\mathbf{P} ::= \mathbf{program\ C}$

$\mathbf{E} ::= \mathbf{B} \mid \mathbf{true} \mid \mathbf{false} \mid \mathbf{read} \mid \mathbf{I} \mid \mathbf{E_1(E_2)}$
$\quad \mid \mathbf{if\ E\ then\ E_1\ else\ E_2} \mid \mathbf{E_1\,O\,E_2}$

$\mathbf{C} ::= \mathbf{E_1 := E_2} \mid \mathbf{output\ E} \mid \mathbf{E_1(E_2)} \mid \mathbf{if\ E\ then\ C_1\ else\ C_2}$
$\quad \mid \mathbf{while\ E\ do\ C} \mid \mathbf{begin\ D;C\ end} \mid \mathbf{C_1;C_2}$

$\mathbf{D} ::= \mathbf{const\ I = E} \mid \mathbf{var\ I = E} \mid \mathbf{proc\ I(I_1);C} \mid \mathbf{fun\ I(I_1);E} \mid \mathbf{D_1;D_2}$

We have procedure (and function) calls of the form $\mathbf{E_1(E_2)}$, rather than just $\mathbf{I(E)}$, to permit calls like $\mathbf{(if\ E_1\ then\ I_1\ else\ I_2)(E_2)}$ in which either the procedure (or function) denoted by $\mathbf{I_1}$ or the one denoted by $\mathbf{I_2}$ is applied to $\mathbf{E_2}$, depending on the value of $\mathbf{E_1}$. Similarly we permit assignments of the form $\mathbf{(if\ E_1\ then\ I_1\ else\ I_2) := E_2}$ or even $\mathbf{I(E_1) := E_2}$ (in which the location assigned to is the result of the function call $\mathbf{I(E_1)}$).

6.2. Semantics of SMALL

6.2.1. Semantic domains

The primitive semantic domains of SMALL are:

Num	The domain of numbers **n**.
Bool	The domain of booleans **b**.
Loc	The domain of locations **ι**.
Bv	The domain of basic values **e**.

Basic values are the denotations of basic constants. If **Bas** = {**0, 1, 2, ...**} then **Bv** = {**0, 1, 2, ...**}—however, for simplicity, we shall not specify any particular choice of basic values or constants.

The compound semantic domains are defined by the following domain equations:

Dv	= **Loc + Rv + Proc + Fun**	—denotable values **d**
Sv	= **File + Rv**	—storable values **v**
Ev	= **Dv**	—expressible values **e**
Rv	= **Bool + Bv**	—R-values **e**
File	= **Rv***	—files **i**
Env	= **Ide→[Dv + {unbound}]**	—environments **r**
Store	= **Loc→[Sv + {unused}]**	—stores **s**
Cc	= **Store→Ans**	—command continuations **c**
Ec	= **Ev→Cc**	—expression continuations **k**
Dc	= **Env→Cc**	—declaration continuations **u**
Proc	= **Cc→Ec**	—procedure values **p**
Fun	= **Ec→Ec**	—function values **f**
Ans	= **{error, stop} + [Rv × Ans]**	—final answers **a**

We assume **Loc** contains a location **input** which holds the input file. We have not provided SMALL with any facilities for creating new files; this is discussed in 9.5. For the time being the only file around is the input.

6.2.2. Semantic functions

We assume as given:

B:**Bas**→**Bv**
O:**Opr**→[**Rv** × **Rv**]→**Ec**→**Cc**

For example, if **Bas** = {**0, 1, 2, ...**}, **Opr** = { + , × , -, /, ...} and **Bv** = **Num** then we might have **B**[**0**] = **0**, **O**[+](**1, 2**)**k** = **k3**, **O**[/](**1, 0**)**k** = **err**, etc.

The meanings of the non-basic constructs are given by:

P:**Pro**→**File**→**Ans**
R:**Exp**→**Env**→**Ec**→**Cc**
E:**Exp**→**Env**→**Ec**→**Cc**
C:**Com**→**Env**→**Cc**→**Cc**
D:**Dec**→**Env**→**Dc**→**Cc**

These are defined by the following semantic clauses.

6.2.3. Semantic clauses

6.2.3.1. Programs

(P) **P[program C] i = C[C]( ) (λs . stop)(i/input)**

The final answer produced when **program C** is run with input **i** is obtained by evaluating the command **C** with an empty environment (**( )** = λ**I . unbound**), a store in which the only used location is **input,** which has contents **i** ((**i/input**) = λι . ι = **input→i, unused**), and a continuation which when sent a store stops with final answer **stop**.

6.2.3.2. Expressions

(R) **R[E] r k = E[E] r;deref;Rv?;k**

E is evaluated, and its result dereferenced and then checked to make sure it is an R-value, which is then passed to the rest of the program.

(E1) **E[B] r k = k(B[B])**

B[B] is passed to the rest of the program.

(E2) **E[true] r k = k true , E[false] r k = k false**

The appropriate boolean value is passed to the rest of the program.

(E3) **E[read] r k s =**
null(s input)→error, k(hd(s input))(s[tl(s input)/input])

If the input file (i.e. **s input**) is empty then an error occurs; otherwise the first item on the input (**hd(s input)**) is sent to the rest of the program, **k**, together with a store in which the item first read has been removed from the input file (**s[tl(s input)/input]**).

(E4) **E[I] r k = (r I = unbound)→err, k(r I)**

If **I** is unbound, an error occurs; otherwise the value denoted by **I** in the environment is sent to the rest of the program.

(E5) **E[E_1(E_2)] r k = E[E_1] r;Fun?λf . E[E_2] r;f;k**

$\mathbf{E_1}$ is evaluated and its value checked to ensure it is a function **f**; **E** is then evaluated and its value is passed to **f**; and finally the result of **f** is passed to the rest of the program **k**.

(E6) **E[if E then E_1 else E_2] r k =**
R[E] r;Bool?;cond(E[E_1] r k,E[E_2] r k)

E is evaluated for its R-value, which is then checked to ensure it is a boolean; then $\mathbf{E_1}$ or $\mathbf{E_2}$ is evaluated, depending on whether **E**'s value was **true** or **false**.

(E7) **E[E_1OE_2] r k =**
R[E_1] rλe_1 . R[E_2] rλe_2 . O[O](e_1,e_2)k

$\mathbf{E_1}$ is evaluated for its R-value $\mathbf{e_1}$, then $\mathbf{E_2}$ is evaluated for its R-value $\mathbf{e_2}$, and finally, the result of doing **O** to $\mathbf{e_1}$ and $\mathbf{e_2}$ is sent to the rest of the program **k**.

6.2.3.3. Commands

(C1) **C[E_1 := E_2] r c =**
E[E_1] r;Loc? λι . R[E_2] r;update ι;c

$\mathbf{E_1}$ is evaluated for its L-value **ι**, then $\mathbf{E_2}$ is evaluated for its R-value which is then stored in **ι**, and the resulting store passed to the rest of the program **c**.

(C2) **C[output E] r c =**
R[E] rλe s . (e, c s)

E is evaluated for its R-value **e** and new store **s**; then **e** is put onto the front of the answer produced when the rest of the program **c** is passed **s**.

(C3) **C[$\mathbf{E_1(E_2)}$] r c =**
E[$\mathbf{E_1}$] r;Proc?λp . E[$\mathbf{E_2}$] r;p;c

$\mathbf{E_1}$ is evaluated and its value checked to ensure it is a procedure **p**; $\mathbf{E_2}$ is then evaluated and its value passed to **p**, and finally the store resulting from **p** is passed to the rest of the program **c**.

(C4) **C[if E then $\mathbf{C_1}$ else $\mathbf{C_2}$] r c =**
R[E] r;Bool?;cond(C[$\mathbf{C_1}$] r c,C[$\mathbf{C_2}$] r c)

E is evaluated for its R-value which is then checked to ensure it is a boolean; then $\mathbf{C_1}$ or $\mathbf{C_2}$ is evaluated, depending on whether **E**'s value was **true** or **false**.

(C5) **C[while E do C] r c =**
R[E] r;Bool?; cond(C[C] r;C[while E do C] r c , c)

E is evaluated for its R-value which is then checked to ensure it is a boolean; then if **E**'s value is **true, C** is evaluated and the resulting store passed to the beginning of **while E do C** again. If **E**'s value is **false** then the rest of the program is immediately done.

(C6) **C[begin D;C end] r c = D[D] rλr′ . C[C] r[r′] c**

D is evaluated to get a little environment **r**′, then **C** is evaluated in **r** updated with **r**′, and then the rest of the program **c** is done.

(C7) **C[$\mathbf{C_1;C_2}$] r c = C[$\mathbf{C_1}$] r;C[$\mathbf{C_2}$] r;c**

$\mathbf{C_1}$ is done, then $\mathbf{C_2}$ is done, and then the rest of the program **c** is done.

6.2.3.4. Declarations

(D1) **D[const I = E] r u = R[E] rλe . u(e/I)**

E is evaluated for its R-value **e** and then the little environment **e/I** is passed to the rest of the program **u**.

(D2) **D[var I = E] r u = R[E] r;ref λι . u(ι/I)**

E is evaluated for its R-value which is then stored in a new location **ι**, and the little environment **ι/I** is passed to the rest of the program **u**.

(D3) **D[proc I(I_1);C] r u = u((λc e . C[C] r[e/I_1] c)/I)**

A little environment, in which the procedure value **λce.C[C] r[e/I_1] c** is bound to **I**, is passed to the rest of the program **u**. When this procedure value is called, the body **C** is evaluated in an environment got from the declaration time environment **r** by binding the actual parameter **e** to the formal parameter **I_1**.

(D4) **D[fun I(I_1);E] r u = u((λk e . E[E] r[e/I_1] k)/I)**

A little environment, in which the function value **λke.E[E] r[e/I_1] k** is bound to **I**, is passed to the rest of the program **u**.

(D5) **D[D_1;D_2] r u = D[D_1] rλr_1 . D[D_2] r[r_1]λr_2 . u(r_1[r_2])**

D_1 is evaluated in **r** to get a little environment **r_1**; then **D_2** is evaluated in **r[r_1]** (i.e. **r** updated with the bindings in **r_1**) to get another little environment **r_2**; and then finally **r_1[r_2]** (the bindings from **D_1** updated with those of **D_2**) are passed to the rest of the program **u**. Notice that **D_2** is evaluated in an environment which contains the effects of **D_1**, and that if **D_1** and **D_2** contain declarations of the same identifier then the result of **D_1;D_2** is the result of **D_2**. For example, **const x = 1;const x = x + 1** would bind **x** to **2**.

6.3. A worked example

To illustrate how the semantics of SMALL works we show how to use it to 'evaluate' **program begin var x = read;output x end** with respect to an initial input file **i** such that **null i = false** and **hd i = 1** (for example **i = 1.2.3...**). We show, as expected, that

P[program begin var x = read;output x end] i = (1, stop)

i.e. **C[begin var x = read;output x end]( )(λs . stop)(i/input) = (1, stop)**

We do the calculation in several stages. First let **r** = **( )**, $\mathbf{s_1}$ = **(i/input)**, $\mathbf{s_2} = \mathbf{s_1}$**[tl i/input]** = **(tl i/input)**; assume ι_2 = **new** $\mathbf{s_2}$, and finally let $\mathbf{s_3} = \mathbf{s_2}[1/\iota_2]$. Then:

(i) **E[read] r k** s_1

$= \mathrm{null}(s_1\ \mathrm{input}) \rightarrow \mathrm{error}, k(\mathrm{hd}(s_1\ \mathrm{input}))(s_1[\mathrm{tl}(s_1\ \mathrm{input})/\mathrm{input}])$ (E3)

$= \mathrm{null}\ i \rightarrow \mathrm{error}, k\,1\,(s_1[\mathrm{tl}\ i/\mathrm{input}])$ (s_1 input = i)

$= k\,1\,s_2$ (null i = false)

(ii) **D[var x = read] r u** s_1

$= (R[\![\mathrm{read}]\!]\,r;\mathrm{ref}\ \lambda\iota\,.\,u(\iota/x))\,s_1$ (D2)

$= (E[\![\mathrm{read}]\!]\,r;\mathrm{deref};\mathrm{Rv?};\mathrm{ref}\ \lambda\iota\,.\,u(\iota/x))\,s_1$ (R)

$= E[\![\mathrm{read}]\!]\,r(\mathrm{deref}(\mathrm{Rv?}(\mathrm{ref}\ \lambda\iota\,.\,u(\iota/x))))\,s_1$ (definition of ;)

$= \mathrm{deref}(\mathrm{Rv?}(\mathrm{ref}\ \lambda\iota\,.\,u(\iota/x)))\,1\,s_2$ (by (i) above)

$= \mathrm{isLoc}\ 1 \rightarrow \ldots, \mathrm{Rv?}(\mathrm{ref}\ \lambda\iota\,.\,u(\iota/x))\,1\,s_2$ (definition of **deref**)

$= \mathrm{Rv?}(\mathrm{ref}\ \lambda\iota\,.\,u(\iota/x))\,1\,s_2$ (isLoc 1 = false)

$= \mathrm{isRv}\ 1 \rightarrow (\mathrm{ref}\ \lambda\iota\,.\,u(\iota/x))\,1\,s_2, \ldots$ (definition of **Rv?**)

$= \mathrm{ref}\ (\lambda\iota\,.\,u(\iota/x))\,1\,s_2$ (isRv 1 = true)

$= \mathrm{new}\ s_2 = \mathrm{error} \rightarrow \mathrm{error},$

$\quad \mathrm{update}\ (\mathrm{new}\ s_2)((\lambda\iota\,.\,u(\iota/x))(\mathrm{new}\ s_2))\,1\,s_2$ (definition of **ref**)

$= \mathrm{update}\ \iota_2\ (u(\iota_2/x))\,1\,s_2$ (new $s_2 = \iota_2$)

$= \mathrm{isSv}\ 1 \rightarrow u(\iota_2/x)(s_2[1/\iota_2]), \mathrm{error}$ (definition of **update**)

$= u(\iota_2/x)(s_2[1/\iota_2])$ (isSv 1 = true)

$= u(\iota_2/x)s_3$ ($s_3 = s_2[1/\iota_2]$)

(iii) **C[begin var x = read;output x end] r c** s_1

$= D[\![\mathrm{var}\ x = \mathrm{read}]\!]\,r(\lambda r'\,.\,C[\![\mathrm{output}\ x]\!]\,r[r']\,c)\,s_1$ (C6)

$= (\lambda r'\,.\,C[\![\mathrm{output}\ x]\!]\,r[r']\,c)\,(\iota_2/x)\,s_3$ (by (ii) above)

$= C[\![\mathrm{output}\ x]\!]\,r[\iota_2/x]\,c\,s_3$

$= R[\![x]\!]\,r[\iota_2/x]\,(\lambda e\,s\,.\,(e,c\,s))\,s_3$ (C2)

$= E[\![x]\!]\,r[\iota_2/x]\,(\mathrm{deref}(\mathrm{Rv?}\ \lambda e\,s\,.\,(e,c\,s)))\,s_3$ (R)

$= \mathrm{deref}(\mathrm{Rv?}\ \lambda e\,s\,.\,(e,c\,s))\,\iota_2\,s_3$ ((E4), $r[\iota_2/x]x = \iota_2$)

$= \mathrm{isLoc}\ \iota_2 \rightarrow \mathrm{cont}(\mathrm{Rv?}\ \lambda e\,s\,.\,(e,c\,s))\,\iota_2\,s_3, \ldots$ (definition of **deref**)

$= \mathrm{cont}(\mathrm{Rv?}\ \lambda e\,s\,.\,(e,c\,s))\,\iota_2\,s_3$

$= (\mathrm{Rv?}\ \lambda e\,s\,.\,(e,c\,s))\,1\,s_3$ (definition of **cont**, isLoc ι_2 = true and $s_3\,\iota_2 = 1$)

$= (\lambda e\,s\,.\,(e,c\,s))\,1\,s_3$ (definition of **Rv?**, isRv 1 = true)

$= (1,c\,s_3)$

(iv) $\mathbf{P}$**[program begin var** x = **read;output x end] i**
  = $\mathbf{C}$**[begin var** x = **read;output x end]( )(**λ**s . stop)(i/input)** (P)
  = **(1,(**λ**s . stop)**s_3**)** (by (iii) above)
  = **(1,stop)**

Calculations like this, though very tedious, are purely mechanical. The Semantics Implementation System (SIS) of Peter Mosses [Mosses] is a computer system which, by automating such calculations, runs programs directly from a denotational semantics. Although the resulting 'implementation' is *very* inefficient it is nevertheless useful for 'debugging semantics' and as an aid to language designers. An implementation package (on DEC tapes) is currently available for PDP 10's from Peter Mosses at Aarhus University, Denmark.

7. Escapes and Jumps

In this chapter we describe various constructs which change the 'flow of control'. From a semantic viewpoint the normal continuation is ignored and control passes to some other one. Constructs of this sort are sometimes called *sequencers*.

7.1. Escapes

Escapes enable one to exit from the middle of a construct and then resume computation at its end.

7.1.1. Escapes from commands

To illustrate escaping from commands, we shall describe a construct related to 'event mechanisms' [Knuth 74; Zahn]. We introduce two new kinds of commands: *traps,* **trap** $\mathbf{C}\,\mathbf{I}_1:\mathbf{C}_1,\ldots,\mathbf{I}_n:\mathbf{C}_n$ **end**, and *escapes,* **escapeto I**. Informally the meaning of these is as follows:

(i) On entering **trap** $\mathbf{C}\;\mathbf{I}_1:\mathbf{C}_1,\ldots,\mathbf{I}_n:\mathbf{C}_n$ **end,** the body **C** is executed. If during the execution of **C** a command **escapeto** $\mathbf{I}_i$ is encountered, then immediately the 'postlude' $\mathbf{C}_i$ is executed, and control passes to the rest of the program.

(ii) If no escapes are encountered, then the effect of the trap is just the effect of its body.

The use of constructs like these has been advocated as a more 'structured' way of exiting from loops and dealing with exceptional conditions than the use of unrestricted jumps. For example, in

```
trap while E do   :
                  :
                  if E1 then escapeto x1 else C1
                  if E2 then escapeto x2 else C2
                  :
                  :
        x1:C1',
        x2:C2'
end
```

if $\mathbf{E}_1$ or $\mathbf{E}_2$ becomes true then the while command is aborted and either

$\mathbf{C}_1{}'$ or $\mathbf{C}_2{}'$ is done.

For the semantics of escapes we simply make the escape identifiers denote continuations defined by the corresponding postludes, and then when **escapeto I** is encountered, the normal continuation is ignored and the one bound to **I** used instead. Thus

$$\mathcal{C}[\textbf{trap}\ \mathbf{C}\ \mathbf{I}_1{:}\mathbf{C}_1,\ldots,\mathbf{I}_n{:}\mathbf{C}_n\ \textbf{end}]\,\mathbf{r}\,\mathbf{c} =$$

$$\mathcal{C}[\mathbf{C}]\,\mathbf{r}[\mathcal{C}[\mathbf{C}_1]\,\mathbf{r}\,\mathbf{c},\ldots,\mathcal{C}[\mathbf{C}_n]\,\mathbf{r}\,\mathbf{c}/\mathbf{I}_1,\ldots,\mathbf{I}_n]\,\mathbf{c}$$

$$\mathcal{C}[\textbf{escapeto}\ \mathbf{I}]\,\mathbf{r}\,\mathbf{c} = \mathcal{E}[\mathbf{I}]\,\mathbf{r};\mathbf{Cc}?\,\lambda\mathbf{c}'.\,\mathbf{c}'$$

This last clause may at first look a bit funny—to see that it is indeed what we want, we have:

$$\begin{aligned}
&\mathcal{C}[\textbf{escapeto}\ \mathbf{I}]\,\mathbf{r}\,\mathbf{c}\,\mathbf{s}\\
&\quad= (\mathcal{E}[\mathbf{I}]\,\mathbf{r};\mathbf{Cc}?\,\lambda\mathbf{c}'.\,\mathbf{c}')\,\mathbf{s}\\
&\quad= \mathcal{E}[\mathbf{I}]\,\mathbf{r}\,(\mathbf{Cc}?\,\lambda\mathbf{c}'.\,\mathbf{c}')\,\mathbf{s}\\
&\quad= (\mathbf{r}\,\mathbf{I} = \mathbf{unbound}) \rightarrow \mathbf{error},\ (\mathbf{Cc}?\,\lambda\mathbf{c}'.\,\mathbf{c}')(\mathbf{r}\,\mathbf{I})\,\mathbf{s}\\
&\quad= (\mathbf{r}\,\mathbf{I} = \mathbf{unbound}) \rightarrow \mathbf{error},\\
&\qquad \mathbf{isCc}(\mathbf{r}\,\mathbf{I}) \rightarrow (\lambda\mathbf{c}'.\,\mathbf{c}')(\mathbf{r}\,\mathbf{I})\,\mathbf{s},\ \mathbf{error}\\
&\quad= (\mathbf{r}\,\mathbf{I} = \mathbf{unbound}) \rightarrow \mathbf{error},\\
&\qquad \mathbf{isCc}(\mathbf{r}\,\mathbf{I}) \rightarrow \mathbf{r}\,\mathbf{I}\,\mathbf{s},\ \mathbf{error}
\end{aligned}$$

Thus if **r I** is bound to a command continuation (as it should be in the body of a trap) then the effect of **escapeto I** is to pass the store to this continuation. As is clear from the clause for traps the continuation bound to **I** will cause the appropriate postlude, and then the rest of the program, to be done. Notice that for these semantic clauses to make sense members of **Cc** must be denotable (i.e. **Dv** = ... + **Cc** + ...).

An iteration construct closely related to this kind of escape is described in 10.2.

7.1.2. Escapes from expressions

An example of an escape mechanism for expressions is Landin's J-operator [Landin] or the jumpout facility in POP-2. To illustrate the essential idea of these we introduce expressions **jumpout I in E** with meaning as follows:

(i) To evaluate **jumpout I in E** one starts evaluating the body **E**. If during **E**'s evaluation a function call $\mathbf{I}(\mathbf{E}_1)$ is encountered then $\mathbf{E}_1$ is evaluated and its value immediately returned as the value of **jumpout I in E**.

(ii) If no call of **I** is encountered then the result of **jumpout I in E** is just the result of **E**.

Thus in the body **E** of **jumpout I in E, I** denoted a 'function-like' value which, when called, immediately returns the value of its actual parameter as the value of **jumpout I in E**. **I** differs from an ordinary function in that it never returns to the point from which it was called. For example

$$\textbf{jumpout I in ((if E then I(E}_1\textbf{) else E}_2\textbf{)} + \textbf{E}_3\textbf{)}$$

is equivalent to

$$\textbf{if E then E}_1 \textbf{ else (E}_2 + \textbf{E}_3\textbf{)}$$

The semantics is straightforward:

$$\mathbf{E}[\![\textbf{jumpout I in E}]\!]\, \mathbf{r}\, \mathbf{k} = \mathbf{E}[\![\mathbf{E}]\!]\, \mathbf{r}[(\lambda \mathbf{e}\, \mathbf{k}' . \mathbf{k}\, \mathbf{e})/\mathbf{I}]\, \mathbf{k}$$

E is evaluated in an environment in which the 'jumpout function' **I** is bound to the function value $\lambda \mathbf{e}\,\mathbf{k}' . \mathbf{k}\,\mathbf{e}$. This function value, when passed an actual parameter **e** and 'return address' **k**′, promptly ignores **k**′ and passes **e** to the rest of the program following **jumpout I in E**.

7.1.3. valof and resultis

A hybrid kind of escape construct occurs in BCPL and PAL. In these, one has an escape trap **valof C** which is an *expression*, though its body **C** is a command. The expression **valof C** is used with the escape *command* **resultis E** as follows:

(i) The value of **valof C** is obtained by evaluating **C** until a **resultis E** is encountered. The value of **valof C** is then the value of **E**.

(ii) If the evaluation of **C** finishes without any **resultis E** being encountered then an error results.

For example, a function **fact** to compute the factorial of **n** could be declared by:

```
fun fact (n);
    valof begin var x = 1;
                while n>0 do (x := n × x;n := n-1);
                resultis x
          end
```

The semantics of **resultis E** is roughly

$$\mathcal{C}[\textbf{resultis E}]\,\mathbf{r}\,\mathbf{c} = \mathcal{R}[\mathbf{E}]\,\mathbf{r}\,\mathbf{k}$$

where **k** is the continuation representing the rest of the program following the enclosing **valof C**. There are two possible ways of handling this **k**:

(i) One can make **k** an argument of the semantic function $\mathcal{C}$—i.e. change the type of $\mathcal{C}$ to:

$$\mathcal{C}:\mathbf{Com}\rightarrow\mathbf{Env}\rightarrow\mathbf{Ec}\rightarrow\mathbf{Cc}\rightarrow\mathbf{Cc}$$

valof continuation (arrow to **Ec**) — normal continuation (arrow to the first **Cc**)

then:

$$\mathcal{C}[\textbf{resultis E}]\,\mathbf{r}\,\mathbf{k}\,\mathbf{c} = \mathcal{R}[\mathbf{E}]\,\mathbf{r}\,\mathbf{k}$$
$$\mathcal{E}[\textbf{valof C}]\,\mathbf{r}\,\mathbf{k} = \mathcal{C}[\mathbf{C}]\,\mathbf{r}\,\mathbf{k}\,\mathbf{err}$$

where the continuation **err** in the last clause is only used if **C** finishes without encountering a **resultis E**. With this approach to handling **k**, one also has to change all the other semantic clauses for commands so that **k** is either passed on or ignored. For example:

$$\mathcal{C}[\textbf{output E}]\,\mathbf{r}\,\mathbf{k}\,\mathbf{c} = \mathcal{R}[\mathbf{E}]\,\mathbf{r}\,\lambda\mathbf{e}\,\mathbf{s}\,.\,(\mathbf{e},\mathbf{c}\,\mathbf{s})$$
$$\mathcal{C}[\mathbf{C}_1;\mathbf{C}_2]\,\mathbf{r}\,\mathbf{k}\,\mathbf{c} = \mathcal{C}[\mathbf{C}_1]\,\mathbf{r}\,\mathbf{k};\mathcal{C}[\mathbf{C}_2]\,\mathbf{r}\,\mathbf{k};\mathbf{c}$$

(ii) One can make **k** part of the environment and redefine

$$\mathbf{Env} = [\mathbf{Ide}\rightarrow[\mathbf{Dv}+\{\mathbf{unbound}\}]]\times\mathbf{Ec}$$

and then

$$\mathbf{C[resultis\ E]\ r\ c\ =\ R[E]\ r;el\ 2\ r}$$
$$\mathbf{E[valof\ C]\ r\ k\ =\ C[C]\ (el\ 1\ r,k)\ err}$$

We must also redefine **E[I]** to handle these new environments:

$$\mathbf{E[I]\ r\ k\ =\ (el\ 1\ r\ I = unbound) \rightarrow error, k(el\ 1\ r\ I)}$$

We discussed these two essentially equivalent methods of treating **valof** and **resultis** to show that sometimes there is not a single, obviously preferred way of doing things. The first method has the advantage that escape continuations are not hidden—so the possibility of escape can immediately be seen from the type of **C**. The second method has the advantage that it expresses the fact that escape continuations are 'statically scoped', just like environments.

7.2 Jumps

Jumps are changes in the flow of control typically invoked by goto commands of the form **goto I**. For example, if **noaction** is a command which does nothing (i.e. **C[noaction] r c = c**) then

L:if E then C;goto L else noaction

is equivalent to **while E do C**. Escapes are restricted jumps in which one can only transfer control to the end of a construct. The semantics of escapes easily generalizes to handle arbitrary jumps. For example:

$$\mathbf{C[goto\ I]\ r\ c\ =\ E[I]\ r;Cc?\ \lambda c'\ .\ c'}$$

This is just like **C[escapeto I]**; general jumps differ not in the semantics of changing the flow of control, but in the places to which control can pass. The only problem is getting the appropriate continuation bound to the corresponding labels. To do this we must:

(i) Determine the *scope* of each label—i.e. the places in the program from which one can jump to it. In PASCAL, labels must occur in procedure bodies and one can only jump between commands in the same body. Thus the scope of a label in PASCAL is the smallest procedure body in which it occurs. In ALGOL 60, on the other hand, the scope of a label is the smallest textually enclosing block. Throughout its scope each label denotes a *fixed* value (a continuation), just as other identifiers do.

(ii) Determine the continuation denoted by each label. For example, in ALGOL 60 one can jump 'into' for-statements and the arms of conditionals, and so if a label occurs in the middle of such a construct then the continuation it denotes is the 'rest of the construct' followed by the 'rest of the program' following the construct. Determining this continuation can be messy—as we shall see.

7.2.1. The semantics of jumps

To illustrate a typical semantics, we add labels and gotos to SMALL. Thus we add to the commands of SMALL **goto I** and **I:C** with meaning such that:

(i) The scope of each label is the smallest textually enclosing **begin**/**end** block.

(ii) One can jump into both the arms of conditionals and the bodies of while commands.

To handle the semantics of this we must ensure that on entering a block **begin D;C end,** we bind to each label occurring in **C** the continuation corresponding to the 'rest of the program' following it. Now this 'rest of the program' is only implicitly defined by the position of the label, and so to extract the appropriate continuation we define a function
$\mathbf{J}:\mathbf{Com}\to\mathbf{Env}\to\mathbf{Cc}\to\mathbf{Env}$ such that

$$\mathbf{J}[\mathbf{C}]\,\mathbf{r}\,\mathbf{c} = (\mathbf{c}_1,\ldots,\mathbf{c}_n/\mathbf{I}_1,\ldots,\mathbf{I}_n)$$

where $\mathbf{I}_1,\ldots,\mathbf{I}_n$ are the labels occurring in **C** and $\mathbf{c}_1,\ldots,\mathbf{c}_n$ the continuations corresponding to them (if **C** is evaluated in environment **r** and with continuation **c**). Thus $\mathbf{c}_i$ is the continuation from $\mathbf{I}_i$ to the 'end of the program' in which the block occurs. This consists of the program from $\mathbf{I}_i$ to the end of the block followed by the 'rest of the program' **c** from the end of the block to the end of the program. Before we define **J**, note that **Com** is now defined by:

$$\mathbf{C} ::= \mathbf{E}_1 := \mathbf{E}_2 \mid \textbf{output}\ \mathbf{E} \mid \mathbf{E}_1(\mathbf{E}_2) \mid \textbf{if}\ \mathbf{E}\ \textbf{then}\ \mathbf{C}_1\ \textbf{else}\ \mathbf{C}_2$$
$$\mid \textbf{while}\ \mathbf{E}\ \textbf{do}\ \mathbf{C} \mid \textbf{begin}\ \mathbf{D};\mathbf{C}\ \textbf{end} \mid \mathbf{C}_1;\mathbf{C}_2 \mid \textbf{goto}\ \mathbf{I} \mid \mathbf{I}:\mathbf{C}$$

Then $\mathbf{J}$ is defined by cases as follows:

$$\mathbf{J}[\mathbf{E_1 := E_2}]\,\mathbf{r}\,\mathbf{c} = \mathbf{J}[\mathbf{output\ E}]\,\mathbf{r}\,\mathbf{c} = \mathbf{J}[\mathbf{E_1(E_2)}]\,\mathbf{r}\,\mathbf{c} = (\,)$$

Since none of these commands can contain labels, $\mathbf{J}$ produces the empty label binding ( ) when applied to them.

$$\mathbf{J}[\mathbf{if\ E\ then\ C_1\ else\ C_2}]\,\mathbf{r}\,\mathbf{c} = \mathbf{J}[\mathbf{C_1}]\,\mathbf{r}\,\mathbf{c}\,[\mathbf{J}[\mathbf{C_2}]\,\mathbf{r}\,\mathbf{c}]$$

The label bindings specified by **if E then** $\mathbf{C_1}$ **else** $\mathbf{C_2}$ are the ones specified by $\mathbf{C_1}$ combined with those specified by $\mathbf{C_2}$. Recall that $\mathbf{r_1}[\mathbf{r_2}]$ is $\mathbf{r_1}$ updated by $\mathbf{r_2}$, so the asymmetry of $\mathbf{J}[\mathbf{C_1}]\,\mathbf{r}\,\mathbf{c}[\mathbf{J}[\mathbf{C_2}]\,\mathbf{r}\,\mathbf{c}]$ reflects an arbitrary decision that if a label occurs in both $\mathbf{C_1}$ and $\mathbf{C_2}$ then it is the one in $\mathbf{C_2}$ that counts. For example

$$\mathbf{goto\ L;if\ E\ then\ L{:}C_1\ else\ L{:}C_2}$$

will cause a jump to $\mathbf{C_2}$. If we had wanted to disambiguate the other way, we would have used $\mathbf{J}[\mathbf{C_2}]\,\mathbf{r}\,\mathbf{c}\,[\mathbf{J}[\mathbf{C_1}]\,\mathbf{r}\,\mathbf{c}]$. Probably the least ad hoc thing to do would be to prohibit more than one occurrence of a label in a given scope. To do this is straightforward but requires a messy syntax.

$$\mathbf{J}[\mathbf{while\ E\ do\ C}]\,\mathbf{r}\,\mathbf{c} = \mathbf{J}[\mathbf{C}]\,\mathbf{r}\,(\mathbf{C}[\mathbf{while\ E\ do\ C}]\,\mathbf{r}\,\mathbf{c})$$

The label bindings specified by **while E do C** are those of **C**, computed with respect to a continuation $\mathbf{C}[\mathbf{while\ E\ do\ C}]\,\mathbf{r}\,\mathbf{c}$, to reflect the fact that after the body of a while is completed, control returns to its beginning.

$$\mathbf{J}[\mathbf{begin\ D;C\ end}]\,\mathbf{r}\,\mathbf{c} = (\,)$$

Since the scope of labels is the block in which they occur, one cannot jump into blocks, and so no label bindings are exported out.

$$\mathbf{J}[\mathbf{C_1;C_2}]\,\mathbf{r}\,\mathbf{c} = \mathbf{J}[\mathbf{C_1}]\,\mathbf{r}\,(\mathbf{C}[\mathbf{C_2}]\,\mathbf{r}\,\mathbf{c})\,[\mathbf{J}[\mathbf{C_2}]\,\mathbf{r}\,\mathbf{c}]$$

The label bindings from $\mathbf{C_1;C_2}$ are those of $\mathbf{C_1}$, computed with respect to the continuation $\mathbf{C}[\mathbf{C_2}]\,\mathbf{r}\,\mathbf{c}$, combined with those of $\mathbf{C_2}$. If a label occurs in both $\mathbf{C_1}$ and $\mathbf{C_2}$ then the one in $\mathbf{C_1}$ is ignored (see the discussion of the conditional).

$$\mathbf{J}[\mathbf{goto\ I}]\,\mathbf{r}\,\mathbf{c} = (\,)$$

goto I cannot contain any labelled commands.

$$\mathbf{J}[\mathbf{I{:}C}]\,\mathbf{r}\,\mathbf{c} = \mathbf{J}[\mathbf{C}]\,\mathbf{r}\,\mathbf{c}\,[\mathbf{C}[\mathbf{C}]\,\mathbf{r}\,\mathbf{c}/\mathbf{I}]$$

I:C gives rise to all the bindings of **C**, together with the new binding **C[C] r c/I**—i.e. **I** is bound to the continuation corresponding to doing **C** then the 'rest of the program' **c**.

Before we describe the use of **J**, note that when *executing* the command **I:C**, the **I** is ignored and hence

$$\mathbf{C[I{:}C] = C[C]}$$

The denotation of **I:C** is identical to that of **C**—the purpose of the "**I:**" is just to mark a place in the program so **J** can extract the appropriate continuation.

We can now use **J** to write a semantic clause for blocks which sets up label bindings:

$$\mathbf{C[begin\ D;C\ end]\ r\ c = D[D]\ r\ \lambda r'\ .\ C[C]\ r[r'][r'']\ c}$$
$$\mathbf{wherered\ r'' = J[C]\ r[r'][r'']\ c}$$

The explanation of why $\mathbf{r''}$ must be recursively defined like this is rather subtle and perhaps best conveyed by an example. Let **C** be the 'infinite loop' **L:output 1;goto L**. It is easy to see from our definition of **J** that:

$$\mathbf{J[C]\ r\ c = J[L{:}output\ 1;goto\ L]\ r\ c = (c_1/L)}$$
$$\mathbf{where\ c_1 = \lambda s\ .\ (1,r\ L\ s)}$$

Now if we just bound $\mathbf{c_1}$ to **L** when evaluating **L:output 1;goto L** then

$$\mathbf{C[L{:}output\ 1;goto\ L]\ r[c_1/L]\ c\ s = (1,(1,r\ L\ s))}$$

so **1** would be output twice and then control would pass out of the loop to **r L**. This is wrong—what we want is to bind to **L** a continuation, $\mathbf{c_2}$ say, which, after it outputs **1**, 'goes back' to $\mathbf{c_2}$ again—and thus repeatedly outputs **1** forever. This is achieved by defining $\mathbf{c_2}$ recursively by $\mathbf{c_2 = \lambda s\ .\ (1,c_2\ s)}$—i.e. defining $\mathbf{(c_2/L) = J[C]\ r[c_2/L]\ c}$, or in other words defining $\mathbf{c_2 = r''\ L}$ where $\mathbf{r'' = J[C]\ r[r'']\ c}$. Then: $\mathbf{C[L{:}output\ 1;goto\ L]\ r[c_2/L]\ c\ s = (1,(1,\ldots)))}$.

Generalizing this argument leads to the requirement that $\mathbf{r'' = J[C]\ r[r'][r'']\ c}$ in the semantic clause for blocks.

The mutually recursive definition of the denotations of labels is not really surprising if one reflects on the fact that in, for example,

```
⋮
L1:goto L2;
⋮
L2:goto L1;
⋮
```

the 'rest of the program' following $\mathbf{L}_1$ starts with the 'rest of the program' following $\mathbf{L}_2$ and the 'rest of the program' following $\mathbf{L}_2$ starts with the 'rest of the program' following $\mathbf{L}_1$.

Summing up, the semantics of jumps is:

$$\mathbf{C}[\![\mathbf{I}{:}\mathbf{C}]\!] = \mathbf{C}[\![\mathbf{C}]\!]$$
$$\mathbf{C}[\![\mathbf{goto\ I}]\!]\,\mathbf{r}\,\mathbf{c} = \mathbf{E}[\![\mathbf{I}]\!]\,\mathbf{r};\mathbf{Cc?}\,\lambda\mathbf{c}'.\,\mathbf{c}'$$
$$\mathbf{C}[\![\mathbf{begin\ D;C\ end}]\!]\,\mathbf{r}\,\mathbf{c} = \mathbf{D}[\![\mathbf{D}]\!]\,\mathbf{r}\,\lambda\mathbf{r}'.\,\mathbf{C}[\![\mathbf{C}]\!]\,\mathbf{r}[\mathbf{r}'][\mathbf{r}'']\,\mathbf{c} \quad \mathbf{whererec}\ \mathbf{r}'' = \mathbf{J}[\![\mathbf{C}]\!]\,\mathbf{r}[\mathbf{r}'][\mathbf{r}'']\,\mathbf{c}$$

Finally, notice that to handle computed goto's such as **goto (if E then L**$_1$ **else L**$_2$**)**, we just replace the construct **goto I** with the more general one, **goto E**, and define

$$\mathbf{C}[\![\mathbf{goto\ E}]\!]\,\mathbf{r}\,\mathbf{c} = \mathbf{R}[\![\mathbf{E}]\!]\,\mathbf{r};\mathbf{Cc?}\,\lambda\mathbf{c}'.\,\mathbf{c}'$$

(we use **R** to cope with the possibility that continuations are the values of variables—this is discussed briefly in the next section).

Note also that we have arbitrarily assumed that labels are identifiers—in some languages (e.g. PASCAL) other things (e.g. numerals) are used. In such cases a special label environment would be needed since label bindings could no longer be held in the ordinary environment.

7.2.2. Assigning label values to variables

In some languages, e.g. PAL [Evans], one can assign labels to variables. For example, when **goto I** is executed in

```
begin
     ⋮
     L:
     ⋮
     I := L;
     ⋮
end;
goto I
```

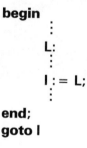

control re-enters the block which has already been left. To handle the semantics of this, all one has to do is to include command continuations in the R-values. The semantic clauses for $\mathbf{E}_1 := \mathbf{E}_2$ and **goto E** described previously will then handle such jumps automatically.

Treating labels as 'first class values' in this way enables powerful control structures like backtracking and co-routines to be implemented. It also makes the language hard to implement efficiently since local storage cannot be reclaimed after exiting from blocks and procedures, as they might be jumped back into later.

8. Various kinds of procedures and functions

In this chapter we discuss a number of 'dimensions' along which procedures (and functions) can be varied. In outline these are:

(i) Number of parameters.
(ii) Possibility of recursion.
(iii) Environment used to bind free identifiers (i.e. identifiers in the body which are not formal parameters).
(iv) Coercion of the actual parameter value.
(v) Evaluation of the actual parameter expression.

8.1. Procedures (or functions) with zero or more parameters

In SMALL, every procedure (and function) had exactly one parameter. Other possibilities are:

8.1.1. Zero parameters

We might have declarations **proc I;C** and **fun I;E** with semantics:

$$\mathcal{D}[\![\mathbf{proc}\ \mathsf{I;C}]\!]\,\mathsf{r\,u} = \mathsf{u(p/I)}$$
$$\text{where } \mathsf{p} = \lambda \mathsf{c}\,.\,\mathcal{C}[\![\mathsf{C}]\!]\,\mathsf{r\,c} = \mathcal{C}[\![\mathsf{C}]\!]\,\mathsf{r}$$
$$\mathcal{D}[\![\mathbf{fun}\ \mathsf{I;E}]\!]\,\mathsf{r\,u} = \mathsf{u(f/I)}$$
$$\text{where } \mathsf{f} = \lambda \mathsf{k}\,.\,\mathcal{E}[\![\mathsf{E}]\!]\,\mathsf{r\,k} = \mathcal{E}[\![\mathsf{E}]\!]\,\mathsf{r}$$

Here **p** and **f** have types **Cc→Cc** and **Ec→Cc** respectively, so we define:

$\mathbf{Proc}_0 = \mathbf{Cc}\to\mathbf{Cc}$ —procedure values of zero parameters
$\mathbf{Fun}_0 = \mathbf{Ec}\to\mathbf{Cc}$ —function values of zero parameters

For the above semantic clauses to make sense, $\mathbf{Proc}_0$ and $\mathbf{Fun}_0$ must be included in (i.e. made summands of) the denotable values **Dv**.
To handle parameterless procedure calls we just add commands of the form **I** and give them semantics:

$$\mathcal{C}[\![\mathsf{I}]\!]\,\mathsf{r\,c} = \mathcal{E}[\![\mathsf{I}]\!]\,\mathsf{r};\mathbf{Proc}_0?\,\lambda \mathsf{p}\,.\,\mathsf{p\,c}$$

Parameterless function calls are slightly trickier since we already have expressions of the form **I**. Two possibilities are:

(i) To syntactically distinguish calls—e.g. give them syntax **I( )**, or, more generally, **E( )**—with semantics:

$$\mathbf{E[E(\,)]\,r\,k = E[E]\,r;Fun_0?\,\lambda f\,.\,f\,k}$$

(ii) To use the expression **I** both for parameterless function calls *and* for naming constants and variables. In this case we must redefine **E[I]** by:

$$\mathbf{E[I]\,r\,k = (r\,I = unbound) \rightarrow err,}$$
$$\mathbf{isFun_0(r\,I) \rightarrow r\,I\,k\,,\,k(r\,I)}$$

8.1.2. More than one parameter

We might have declarations **proc** $\mathbf{I(I_1,I_2);C}$, **proc** $\mathbf{I(I_1,I_2,I_3);C}$, ... etc., and **fun** $\mathbf{I(I_1,I_2);E}$, **fun** $\mathbf{I(I_1,I_2,I_3);E}$, ... etc., with semantics

$$\mathbf{D[proc\ I(I_1,\ldots,I_n);C]\,r\,u = u(p/I)}$$
$$\mathbf{where\ p = \lambda c(e_1,\ldots,e_n)\,.\,C[C]\,r[e_1,\ldots,e_n/I_1,\ldots,I_n]\,c}$$

$$\mathbf{D[fun\ I(I_1,\ldots,I_n);E]\,r\,u = u(f/I)}$$
$$\mathbf{where\ f = \lambda k(e_1,\ldots,e_n)\,.\,E[E]\,r[e_1,\ldots,e_n/I_1,\ldots,I_n]\,k}$$

For each **n**, we need domains $\mathbf{Proc_n}$ and $\mathbf{Fun_n}$ for procedure and function values with **n** parameters:

$$\mathbf{Proc_n = Cc \rightarrow Ev^n \rightarrow Cc}$$
$$\mathbf{Fun_n = Ec \rightarrow Ev^n \rightarrow Cc}$$

Then for the above semantic clauses to make sense we must make all these procedure and function values denotable, i.e.

$$\mathbf{Dv = \ldots + Proc_1 + Proc_2 + \ldots + Fun_1 + Fun_2 + \ldots}$$

For calling we use the syntax $\mathbf{E(E_1,\ldots,E_n)}$ with semantics

$$\mathbf{C[E(E_1,\ldots,E_n)]\,r\,c =}$$
$$\mathbf{E[E]\,r;Proc_n?\,\lambda p\,.\,E[E_1]\,r\,\lambda e_1\,.\ldots E[E_n]\,r\,\lambda e_n\,.\,p\,c\,(e_1,\ldots,e_n)}$$

$$\mathbf{E[E(E_1,\ldots,E_n)]\,r\,k =}$$
$$\mathbf{E[E]\,r;Fun_n?\,\lambda f\,.\,E[E_1]\,r\,\lambda e_1\,.\ldots E[E_n]\,r\,\lambda e_n\,.\,f\,k\,(e_1,\ldots,e_n)}$$

Thus the actual parameters are evaluated from left to right. Other orders of parameter evaluation would correspond to other orders of $\mathbf{E[E_1]}$, ...,

$\mathbf{E[E_n]}$ in the right hand side of the semantic clauses.

8.2. Recursive procedures and functions

Consider the following SMALL procedure, **copy**:

> **proc** copy(n);
> **if** n = 0 **then output** 0 **else** (**output read**;copy (n-1))

The idea is that a call **copy(n)** will be equivalent to

$$\underbrace{\textbf{output read;output read;}\ldots\textbf{;output read;}}_{\mathbf{n}\text{ output commands}}\textbf{output 0}$$

so that **n** items will be copied from the input to the output, and then **0** will be printed. Unfortunately, according to the semantics we have given so far, this will not work. To see why not, recall that:

$$\mathbf{D[proc\ I(I_1);C]\ r\ u\ =\ u((\lambda c\ e\ .\ C[C]\ r[e/I_1]\ c)/I)}$$

Thus the environment in which procedure bodies are done—$\mathbf{r[e/I_1]}$—only differs from the declaration time environment **r** in that the actual parameter value **e** is bound to the formal parameter $\mathbf{I_1}$. Thus in the body the procedure name **I** denotes whatever it is bound to in **r**—i.e. whatever **I** happens to be bound to before the declaration. For example, the effect of the command:

> **begin** **proc** copy(n);**output** n;
> **proc** copy(n);**if** n = 0 **then output** 0 **else**
> (**output read**;copy(n-1));
> copy(10)
> **end**

would be to output the first item on the input, then to output **9** and then to stop. The 'recursive' call **copy(n-1)** in the body of the second version of **copy** would be a call to the first version.

To model recursive procedures we must bind the procedure value being declared to its name in its body. If we use $\mathbf{rec\ proc\ I(I_1);C}$ for recursive procedure declarations and retain $\mathbf{proc\ I(I_1);C}$ for non-recursive ones then the semantics are:

$$\mathbf{D[proc\ I(I_1);C]\ r\ u = u(p/I)}$$
$$\mathbf{where\ p = \lambda c\ e\ .\ C[C]\ r[e/I_1]\ c}$$

$$\mathbf{D[rec\ proc\ I(I_1);C]\ r\ u = u(p/I)}$$
$$\mathbf{whererec\ p = \lambda c\ e\ .\ C[C]\ r[p,e/I,I_1]\ c}$$

N.B.

In both PASCAL and ALGOL 60 all procedures are recursive, but in general this need not be so.

To handle the declaration of several mutually recursive procedures we could introduce the construct:

$$\begin{array}{l} \mathbf{rec\ proc\ I_1(I_{1\,1});C_1} \\ \mathbf{and proc\ I_2(I_{2\,1});C_2} \\ \quad\vdots \\ \mathbf{and proc\ I_n(I_{n\,1});C_n} \end{array}$$

with semantics

$$\begin{array}{l} \mathbf{D[rec\ proc\ I_1(I_{1\,1});C_1} \\ \quad \mathbf{and\ proc\ I_2(I_{2\,1});C_2} \\ \qquad\vdots \\ \quad \mathbf{and\ proc\ I_n(I_{n\,1});C_n]r\ u = u(p_1,p_2,\ldots,p_n/I_1,I_2,\ldots,I_n)} \\ \qquad \mathbf{whererec\ p_1 = \lambda c_1 e_1\ .\ C[C_1]r[e_1,p_1,p_2,\ldots,p_n/I_{1\,1},I_1,I_2,\ldots,I_n]\ c_1} \\ \qquad\quad \mathbf{and\quad p_2 = \lambda c_2 e_2\ .\ C[C_2]r[e_2,p_1,p_2,\ldots,p_n/I_{2\,1},I_1,I_2,\ldots,I_n]\ c_2} \\ \qquad\quad\vdots \\ \qquad\quad \mathbf{and\quad p_n = \lambda c_n e_n\ .\ C[C_n]r[e_n,p_1,p_2,\ldots,p_n/I_{n\,1},I_1,I_2,\ldots,I_n]\ c_n} \end{array}$$

Recursive functions **rec fun** $\mathbf{I(I_1);E}$ can be handled analogously to recursive procedures:

$$\mathbf{D[fun\ I(I_1);E]\ r\ u = u(f/I)}$$
$$\mathbf{where\ f = \lambda k\ e\ .\ E[E]\ r[e/I_1]\ k}$$

$$\mathbf{D[rec\ fun\ I(I_1);E]\ r\ u = u(f/I)}$$
$$\mathbf{wherered\ f = \lambda k\ e\ .\ E[E]\ r[f,e/I,I_1]\ k}$$

N.B.

8.2.1. Recursive functions in ALGOL 60 and PASCAL

In both ALGOL 60 and PASCAL, the bodies of functions are commands (not expressions), and the results are returned by assigning to the functions' name. For example, in PASCAL, a squaring function could be defined by:

function square (n:real):real;begin square: = n × n end

An initially plausible semantics, to handle functions which return results in this way, is as follows:

(i) The function name is made to denote a new location (initialized to **unassigned,** say) within its body.
(ii) When control leaves the function body the location denoted by its name has its contents passed as the result of the call. If this contents is still **unassigned,** an error occurs.

It is routine (but messy) to write a semantic clause which expresses this, and we leave it as an exercise for the reader. Notice however that this approach cannot be combined with the semantics of recursive functions discussed in the previous section since the function name would have to be bound to *both* a function value (to handle recursive calls) and a location (to handle the returning of results). To cope with recursive functions we would have to distinguish result-returning assignments—i.e. assignments to the function name—from ordinary ones. The former could then (for example) be treated as assignments to some 'system variable'. To write a semantics modelling this would be straightforward but very messy—the messiness of the semantics reflecting the messiness of the construct.

8.3. Static and dynamic binding

In some languages (for example, LISP and POP-2) procedure (or function) bodies are evaluated in the *call time* rather than the *declaration time* environment. This is called *dynamic binding,* to distinguish it from the *static binding* of ALGOL 60 and PASCAL (and SMALL). In implementation terms, dynamic binding corresponds to using the 'dynamic chain' for looking up identifiers—no 'static chain' is needed.

An example illustrating the difference between the two kinds of binding is:

```
begin  const x = 1;
       proc p(y);output (x+y);
       begin const x = 2;
             p(3)
       end
end
```

With static binding, **1 + 3 = 4** is output, whereas with dynamic binding, **2 + 3 = 5** is output. To see this, note that when **p** is declared, **x = 1,** but when **p** is called, **x = 2**.

8.3.1. Semantics of binding

To describe the semantics of dynamic binding we simply change procedure values so they can be passed the call time environment and change the semantic clause for calling to pass it (functions are analogous to procedures and so we shall not bother to discuss them). Thus:

$$\mathbf{Proc} = \mathbf{Env} \rightarrow \mathbf{Cc} \rightarrow \mathbf{Ec}$$

$$\mathbf{D}[\textbf{proc } \mathbf{I}(\mathbf{I}_1);\mathbf{C}]\,\mathbf{r}\,\mathbf{u} = \mathbf{u}((\lambda \underset{\substack{\nwarrow\\ \text{N.B.}}}{\mathbf{r}'}\,\mathbf{c}\,\mathbf{e}\,.\,\mathbf{C}[\mathbf{C}]\,\underset{\substack{\nearrow\\ \text{N.B.}}}{\mathbf{r}'}[\mathbf{e}/\mathbf{I}_1]\,\mathbf{c})/\mathbf{I})$$

$$\mathbf{C}[\mathbf{E}_1(\mathbf{E}_2)]\,\mathbf{r}\,\mathbf{c} = \mathbf{E}[\mathbf{E}_1]\,\mathbf{r};\mathbf{Proc}?\,\lambda\mathbf{p}\,.\,\mathbf{E}[\mathbf{E}_2]\,\mathbf{r};\mathbf{p}\,\underset{\substack{\uparrow\\ \text{N.B.}}}{\mathbf{r}}\,\mathbf{c}$$

More generally one can imagine procedures whose bodies are evaluated in a mixture of the declaration and call time environments. For example, for any function **mix:Env × Env→Env** we could have procedures defined by:

$$\mathbf{D[proc\ I(I_1);C]\ r\ u = u((\lambda r'\ c\ e\ .\ C[C]\ mix(r,r')[e/I_1]\ c)/I)}$$

Static and dynamic binding are special cases of this:

(i) Static binding corresponds to **mix** = λ(**r**,**r**′) . **r**
(ii) Dynamic binding corresponds to **mix** = λ(**r**,**r**′) . **r**′.

An example of a language with a non-trivial **mix** function is INTERLISP, in which **mix** depends on the 'alist' parameter to the function **FUNCTION**—**(FUNCTION F (**X_1**...**X_n**))** creates a function value with $X_1,\ldots,X_n$ bound statically and all other free identifiers bound dynamically; i.e.

$$\mathbf{mix} = \lambda(r,r')\ .\ r'[r\,X_1,\ldots,r\,X_n/X_1,\ldots,X_n]$$

(N.B. This discussion of INTERLISP is oversimplified and approximate!)

8.3.2. Advantages and disadvantages of dynamic binding

The main advantages of dynamic binding are:

(i) With dynamic binding, recursion works automatically. Since procedure calls occur in the scope of their declaration, the call time environment will include the binding of the procedure's name to its value. Put another way: by the time calls are done, the procedure is already bound to its name, and so recursive calls work.
(ii) Procedures can be written 'top down'—i.e. one can write procedures which call as yet undefined subprocedures. Parts of the main program which do not use the undefined subprocedures can be run directly.
(iii) On-line interactive modification and debugging is easy. If a procedure is redefined, there is no need to recompile all programs which use it. Procedures may thus be 'traced' by temporarily redefining them to print their arguments on entry and result on exit.

For reasons such as these, many interactive languages use dynamic binding. The main disadvantages of it are:

(iv) It is impossible to do compile-time type checking since at compile time one cannot determine what are the types of the things to which free identifiers in procedures will be bound.

(v) Subtle and elusive 'bugs' can appear as a result of procedures or functions being called in contexts in which some of their free identifiers have been rebound. One cannot protect procedure definitions against subsequent inadvertent corruption.
(vi) The conceptual distinction between formal parameters and free identifiers is blurred since all binding is done at call time.

On the whole, people seem to feel that the disadvantages of dynamic binding outweigh the advantages—especially as most of the advantages can be obtained with a statically bound language if a good compiler and debugger are available.

8.4. Parameter passing mechanisms

In SMALL, the undereferenced value of the actual parameter is bound directly to a procedure's formal parameter. This is somewhat similar to PASCAL's call by reference (the differences are discussed below). In other languages various transformations are done to the actual parameter's value before it is bound to the formal parameter. We shall call such transformations *parameter passing* mechanisms and discuss below the main mechanisms that commonly occur.

8.4.1. Call by value

Call by value, as discussed here, is found in most common languages, including ALGOL 60 and PASCAL. The value of the actual parameter is first dereferenced, the resulting R-value is then stored in a new location (local to the procedure body), and finally, this new location is bound to the formal parameter. For example, consider

```
begin proc P(x);x: = 1;
          var x = 2;
          P(x);
          output x
end
```

In SMALL, the call **P(x)** would simply assign **1** to the variable bound to **x** and so **1** would be output. In ALGOL 60 or PASCAL (with **x** called by value) the variable bound to **x** in the body of **P** would be different from the one bound by the declaration **var** x=**2**. Thus no side effect would occur and **2** would be output.

To model call by value we must arrange that inside a procedure's body, the formal parameter denotes a new reference to the dereferenced actual parameter value. This can be described in at least three ways:

(i) The semantic clause for procedure calling can do the necessary dereferencing and creation of a new location, and then pass this new location to the procedure value which binds it directly.

$$\begin{aligned}&\mathbf{C}[\![E_1(E_2)]\!]\,r\,c = \\ &\quad \mathbf{E}[\![E_1]\!]\,r;\mathrm{Proc?}\,\lambda p\,.\,\mathbf{E}[\![E_2]\!]\,r;\mathrm{deref};\mathrm{ref};p\,c\\ &\mathbf{D}[\![\mathbf{proc}\ I(I_1);C]\!]\,r\,u = u(p/I)\\ &\qquad\qquad \text{where } p = \lambda c\,e\,.\,\mathbf{C}[\![C]\!]\,r[e/I_1]\,c\end{aligned}$$

(ii) The procedure value can do the dereferencing and creation of a new location—in this case the semantic clause for procedure calling would just pass the undereferenced actual parameter value.

$$\begin{aligned}&\mathbf{C}[\![E_1(E_2)]\!]\,r\,c = \mathbf{E}[\![E_1]\!]\,r;\mathrm{Proc?}\,\lambda p\,.\,\mathbf{E}[\![E_2]\!]\,r;p\,c\\ &\mathbf{D}[\![\mathbf{proc}\ I(I_1);C]\!]\,r\,u = u(p/I)\\ &\qquad\qquad \text{where } p = \lambda c\,.\,\mathrm{deref};\mathrm{ref}\,\lambda e\,.\,\mathbf{C}[\![C]\!]\,r[e/I_1]\,c\end{aligned}$$

(iii) The semantic clause for procedure calling could do the dereferencing, and the procedure value the allocation of a new location:

$$\begin{aligned}&\mathbf{C}[\![E_1(E_2)]\!]\,r\,c = \mathbf{E}[\![E_1]\!]\,r;\mathrm{Proc?}\,\lambda p\,.\,\mathbf{E}[\![E_2]\!]\,r;\mathrm{deref};p\,c\\ &\mathbf{D}[\![\mathbf{proc}\ I(I_1);C]\!]\,r\,u = u(p/I)\\ &\qquad\qquad \text{where } p = \lambda c\,.\,\mathrm{ref}\,\lambda e\,.\,\mathbf{C}[\![C]\!]\,r[e/I_1]\,c\end{aligned}$$

For languages like ALGOL 60 and PASCAL, each of these three approaches would be equivalent since procedures are always entered immediately after being called. In other languages, POP-2 and SL5 [Hanson], for example, it is possible to bind a procedure to its actual parameters but not execute the body. The execution of the resulting 'closure' can then be invoked separately—perhaps much later. In cases like this, each of the three semantics above is different:

(i) With this, dereferencing and storage allocation (via **ref**) occur at parameter binding time, so if they cause errors, the program will stop then.

(ii) With this, dereferencing and storage allocation are done not when the actual parameters are bound, but when the resulting closure is executed—thus errors will occur then.

(iii) With this, dereferencing errors would manifest themselves at parameter binding time, and allocation errors at closure execution time.

In fact, in POP-2, everything is done when the parameters are bound (as in (i) above), whereas in SL5, everything is done when the procedure body is executed (as in (ii) above). Thus, which of these three descriptions to use in general depends on the language being described. When they are equivalent—as with ALGOL 60 and PASCAL—we shall adopt approach (ii) for the following two reasons:

(a) The parameter passing mechanism is usually specified in the procedure declaration (for example in PASCAL
procedure p(var x:real)... for variable parameters and
procedure p(x:real)... for value parameters). Thus conceptually the semantics of parameter passing should be embedded in the procedure value

(b) It is nice to have a single semantic clause for procedure calls, namely:

$$\mathbf{C}[\![\mathbf{E}_1(\mathbf{E}_2)]\!]\,\mathbf{r}\,\mathbf{c} = \mathbf{E}[\![\mathbf{E}_1]\!]\,\mathbf{r};\mathbf{Proc?}\,\lambda\mathbf{p}\,.\,\mathbf{E}[\![\mathbf{E}_2]\!]\,\mathbf{r};\mathbf{p}\,\mathbf{c}$$

If we put the semantics of parameter passing into the semantic clause for calls then we would require a messy cases switch in its right hand side, for example:

$$\begin{aligned}&\mathbf{C}[\![\mathbf{E}_1(\mathbf{E}_2)]\!]\,\mathbf{r}\,\mathbf{c} =\\ &\quad \mathbf{E}[\![\mathbf{E}_1]\!]\,\mathbf{r};\mathbf{Proc?}\,\lambda\mathbf{p}\,.\,\mathbf{varparameter}\ \mathbf{p}\rightarrow\mathbf{E}[\![\mathbf{E}_2]\!]\,\mathbf{r};\mathbf{p}\,\mathbf{c},\\ &\qquad\qquad\qquad\qquad\quad \mathbf{valueparameter}\ \mathbf{p}\rightarrow\mathbf{E}[\![\mathbf{E}_2]\!]\,\mathbf{r};\mathbf{deref};\mathbf{ref};\mathbf{p}\,\mathbf{c}\\ &\qquad\qquad\qquad\qquad\qquad\qquad\qquad\quad \vdots\end{aligned}$$

As we shall see in the section on calling mechanisms this sort of thing is sometimes inevitable—however when it can be avoided we shall do so.

(a) and (b) above are typical of the sort of 'reasoning' one often has to use to decide between equivalent formal descriptions. The decision must be based on judgements both of conceptual appropriateness (e.g. (a)) and technical convenience (e.g. (b)).

8.4.2. Call by reference

We shall use the phrase *call by reference* for any parameter passing mechanism in which *if* the actual parameter value is a location *then* it is bound directly (i.e. undereferenced) to the formal parameter. Different kinds of call by reference correspond to different actions taken when the actual parameter value is *not* a location.

8.4.2.1. Simple call by reference

With simple call by reference the actual parameter value is bound directly to the formal parameter—nothing is done if this value is not a location. This is the parameter passing method of SMALL and is described by:

$$\mathbf{D}[\![\textbf{proc I(I}_1\textbf{);C}]\!]\,\mathbf{r}\,\mathbf{u} = \mathbf{u(p/I)}$$
$$\textbf{where p} = \lambda\mathbf{c\,e}\,.\,\mathbf{C}[\![\mathbf{C}]\!]\,\mathbf{r[e/I_1]\,c}$$

8.4.2.2. PASCAL call by reference

Formal parameters of PASCAL can be decorated with **var** as in **procedure P(var x:real)....** In this case the value of the corresponding actual parameter must be a location (if not, an error results) which is bound directly. The semantics is thus:

$$\mathbf{D}[\![\textbf{proc I(I}_1\textbf{);C}]\!]\,\mathbf{r}\,\mathbf{u} = \mathbf{u(p/I)}$$
$$\textbf{where p} = \lambda\mathbf{c}\,.\,\mathbf{Loc?}\,\lambda\iota\,.\,\mathbf{C}[\![\mathbf{C}]\!]\,\mathbf{r[\iota/I_1]\,c}$$

8.4.2.3. FORTRAN call by reference

In (some implementations of) FORTRAN, parameters are passed in the following way:

(i) If the value of the actual parameter is a location then this is bound directly to the formal parameter.

(ii) If the value of the actual parameter is not a location then a new location containing it is bound to the formal parameter.

This differs from PASCAL call by reference because of (ii)—in PASCAL, an error would occur. The semantics of FORTRAN call by reference is:

$$\begin{aligned}&\mathbf{D[proc\ I(I_1);C]\ r\ u\ =\ u(p/I)}\\&\qquad\mathbf{where\ p\ =\ \lambda c\,.\,fortran\ \lambda\iota\,.\,C[C]\ r[\iota/I_1]\ c}\\&\qquad\quad\mathbf{where\ fortran\ =\ \lambda k\ e\,.\,isLoc\ e{\to}k\ e,ref\ k\ e}\end{aligned}$$

The function **fortran:Ec→Ec** takes a continuation **k** and produces a continuation which when sent a value **e**, tests it to see if it is a location; if so it sends it straight on to **k**; otherwise it sends a reference to **e** to **k**.

8.4.3. Call by value and result

In this parameter passing method:

(i) The actual parameter value **e** must be a location.
(ii) Inside the procedure body the formal parameter denotes a new location, **ι** say, containing the contents of **e**.
(iii) On leaving the procedure the contents of **ι** is copied into **e**.

This is called call by value and result since (i) and (ii) are similar to call by value (with the extra requirement that the actual parameter value must be a location) and (iii) is sometimes known as call by result. The semantics is routine but slightly messy:

$$\begin{aligned}&\mathbf{D[proc\ I(I_1);C]\ r\ u\ =\ u(p/I)}\\&\ \mathbf{where\ p\ =\ \lambda c\ e\,.\,(Loc?;deref;ref\ \lambda\iota\,.\,C[C]\ r[\iota/I_1]\ (cont(update\ e\ c)\iota))\ e}\end{aligned}$$

The definition of **p** has the form **λc e . (...e...)e**—we cannot cancel the **e's** because of the inner occurrence (in **update e c**).

The purpose of call by value and result is to *simultaneously* gain advantages of both call by reference and call by value. Call by reference has the virtue that results can be returned via formal parameters; with call by value this does not work but, as compensation, the dangers of inadvertent sharing are eliminated. For example, consider the following program to compute the factorial of **n**, and place the result in the location denoted by **res**.

```
proc fact (n,res);
      res: = 1;
      while not (n = 0) do (res: = n × res;n: = n-1)
```

This program has a lurking bug: suppose one calls **fact (x,x)** (hoping to replace **x**'s value by its factorial)—then things will go wrong. Inside the call **fact (x,x)**, both **n** and **res** will denote the location denoted by **x**; thus the initialization **res: = 1** will also set the value of **n** to **1**, and the result of the call will, after one iteration, be to assign **0** as the contents of this location. Thus **fact (x,x)** is equivalent to **x: = 0**!

If we used call by value and result on **fact** then things would work as planned since the effect of a call **fact (x,x)** would be that

(i) New locations, each initialized to **x**'s R-value, would be bound to **n** and **res**.
(ii) The initialization **res: = 1** would only affect the location bound to **res**.
(iii) The **while** command would correctly build up **n!** in **res**.

Thus with call by value and result, we get the best of both worlds—the ability to return results via parameters and the security of call by value. This has to be balanced against the ugly and ad hoc nature of the mechanisms.

8.5. Procedure calling mechanisms

In the previous section we assumed that when a procedure is called, the first thing that happens is that the actual parameter is evaluated. Thus:

$$\mathcal{C}[\mathbf{E_1(E_2)}]\,\mathbf{r\,c} = \mathcal{E}[\mathbf{E_1}]\,\mathbf{r;Proc?}\,\lambda\mathbf{p}\,.\,\mathcal{E}[\mathbf{E_2}]\,\mathbf{r;p\,c}$$

In many languages there are kinds of procedures which, when called, do not 'fully evaluate' the actual parameter. Examples we shall discuss later are ALGOL 60 call by name and LISP FEXPRs. The general shape of the semantics of such a call is:

$$\mathcal{C}[\mathbf{E_1(E_2)}]\,\mathbf{r\,c} = \mathcal{E}[\mathbf{E_1}]\,\mathbf{r;Proc?}\,\lambda\mathbf{p}\,.\,\mathbf{p\,c}\,(\text{'partially evaluated }\mathbf{E_2}\text{'})$$

The evaluation of the actual parameter $\mathbf{E_2}$ is completed each time the formal parameter denoting it is encountered during the execution of the procedure's body.

Before getting down to details a note on our terminology is appropriate. For us, *procedure calling* is the processing of the actual parameter expression to yield some (partially or fully evaluated) value, whereas *parameter passing* is the further processing of this value to yield whatever is eventually bound to the formal parameter. Different procedure calling methods are modelled via different semantic clauses for procedure calls, whereas (as we saw in the last section) different parameter passing methods correspond to different procedure values, and so are modelled with different semantic clauses for procedure declarations. It would, perhaps, have been better to have given the various parameter passing methods names such as "pass by value" or "pass by reference" and so have been able to use "call by" exclusively for calling methods—however we defer to convention. The reader should note that our terminology is not always standard, though.

8.5.1. Call by closure (ALGOL 60 call by name)

With this, the *closure* **E[E₂] r** of the actual parameter $\mathbf{E_2}$ in the call time environment **r** is passed. The semantics of calls is thus:

$$\mathbf{C[E_1(E_2)]\,r\,c = E[E_1]\,r;Proc?\,\lambda p\,.\,p\,c\,(E[E_2]\,r)}$$

$\mathbf{E[E_2]\,r}$ has type **Ec→Cc**; hence we define the domain **Closure** of closures by:

$$\mathbf{Closure = Ec \rightarrow Cc}$$

Closures are usually implemented using parameterless functions called "thunks"; thus it is not surprising that the denotation of closures has the same type as that of parameterless functions.($\mathbf{Closure = Fun_0}$—see 8.1.1.).

With call by closure, closures must be made denotable, and the semantic clause defining **E[I]** must be fixed so that if **I** denotes a closure then it is evaluated. Thus

$$\begin{aligned}\mathbf{E[I]\,r\,k} &= \mathbf{(r\,I = unbound) \rightarrow err,}\\ &\quad \mathbf{isClosure\,(r\,I) \rightarrow r\,I\,k, k(r\,I)}\end{aligned}$$

This ensures that when a formal parameter bound to a closure is encountered in the procedure body, the corresponding closure is evaluated. Notice that this clause is similar to that required for parameterless function calls.

As an example, consider:

begin proc P(x);(**output** x;**output** x);
    P(**read**)
end

If **P** is called by closure then if **r** is the call time environment, $\mathcal{E}$[**read**] **r** is bound to **x**, and so at call time, no reading is done. During the execution of **P**'s body, each evaluation of **x** will cause $\mathcal{E}$[**read**] **r** to be evaluated, and thus the two occurrences of **output x** will cause the first two items from the input to be output. If call by value had been used then at call time the first item on the input would have been read and bound to **x**, and then this would have been output twice.

8.5.2. Call by text (LISP FEXPRs)

With this the *text* $E_2 \varepsilon Exp$ of the actual parameter is passed and thus the semantics is:

$$\mathcal{C}[E_1(E_2)]\,r\,c \;=\; \mathcal{E}[E_1]\,r;Proc?\,\lambda p\,.\,p\,c\,E_2$$

Formal parameters can now denote members of **Exp** and so these must be included in the denotable values **Dv**. To ensure that when text-denoting formal parameters are evaluated, the corresponding expression text is evaluated, we must define:

$$\begin{aligned}\mathcal{E}[I]\,r\,k \;=\; &(r\,I = unbound) \rightarrow err,\\ &isExp(r\,I) \rightarrow \mathcal{E}[r\,I]\,r\,k, k(r\,I)\end{aligned}$$

Notice that with call by text, the environment in which actual parameters are eventually evaluated depends on where the corresponding formal parameters occur in the procedure body and so might vary. With call by closure this environment is fixed as the call time one. To illustrate this, consider:

begin const x=1;
    proc P(y);**begin const** x=2;**output** y **end**;
    P(x)
end

If **P** is called by text **y** will be bound to **x** in **P**, and since when the command **output y** is executed **x** denotes **2**, **2** will be output. With call by closure **E[x] r** would be bound to **y** where **r** is the call time environment in which **x** denotes **1**; when **output y** is done **E[x] r** is evaluated yielding **x**'s value in **r**—i.e. **1**—which is then output.

8.5.3. Call by denotation

With this the *denotation* $\mathbf{E[E_2]}$ of the actual parameter is passed, thus:

$$\mathbf{C[E_1(E_2)]\,r\,c = E[E_1]\,r;Proc?\,\lambda p\,.\,p\,c\,(E[E_2])}$$

Formal parameters can now denote members of **Ed** = **Env→Ec→Cc** (since $\mathbf{E[E_2]}\varepsilon\mathbf{Ed}$) which must therefore be included in the denotable values. We must also ensure that denotations denoting formal parameters get evaluated when used, thus:

$$\begin{aligned}\mathbf{E[I]\,r\,k} &= \mathbf{(r\,I = unbound) \to err,}\\ &\quad\mathbf{isEd(r\,I) \to r\,I\,r\,k, k(r\,I)}\end{aligned}$$

The difference between call by text and denotation is fairly subtle since, as we have described them, they would yield identical final answers. If we did not always force the evaluation of texts and denotations, i.e. if we reverted to

$$\mathbf{E[I]\,r\,k = (r\,I = unbound) \to err, k(r\,I)}$$

then texts, but not denotations, could be subjected to various syntactic processes like compiling, optimising, etc., e.g.

proc run(x);eval (optimise x);

where

$$\mathbf{E[eval\ E]\,r\,k = E[E]\,r;Exp?\,\lambda e\,.\,E[e]\,r\,k}$$

All one could do with denotations would be to 'run' them; for example, using **run E** where:

$$\mathbf{E[run\ E]\,r\,k = E[E]\,r;Ed?\,\lambda e\,.\,e\,r\,k}$$

8.5.4. Quotation constructs

Consider expressions **text E**, **denotation E** and **closure E**, with semantics:

E[text E] r k = k(E)
E[denotation E] r k = k(E[E])
E[closure E] r k = k(E[E] r)

Using these we can simulate the various ways of calling a procedure **P** on actual parameter **E** as follows:

call by text:	**P(text E)**
call by denotation:	**P(denotation E)**
call by closure:	**P(closure E)**

In LISP the expressions **(QUOTE E)**, **(COMPILE E)** and **(FUNCTION E)** correspond *roughly* to **text E**, **denotation E** and **closure E**.

8.6. Summary of calling and passing mechanisms

Gathering together the various mechanisms discussed in the previous two sections we see that the general sequence of events when a procedure is invoked is:

At call time: The actual parameter is evaluated to some degree and passed to the procedure. At this time the distinction between calls by text, denotation and closure is made.

At entry time: The value passed to the procedure is transformed to a denotable value to be bound to the formal parameter. At this time the distinction between calls by value and reference is made.

At execution time: The body of the procedure is executed. If any formal parameters denote texts, denotations or closures then it is during this execution that they are evaluated.

At exit time: The store resulting from the execution of the body is possibly transformed (for example, with call by value and result) and then passed to the continuation following the call.

The general form of the semantics is

$$\mathcal{C}[\mathbf{E_1(E_2)}]\,\mathbf{r\,c} = \mathcal{E}[\mathbf{E_1}]\,\mathbf{r;Proc?}\,\lambda\mathbf{p}\,.\,\mathbf{call\ p\ c\ E_2\ r}$$

$$\mathcal{D}[\mathbf{proc\ I(I_1);C}]\,\mathbf{r\,u} = \mathbf{u(p/I)}$$
$$\mathbf{where\ p} = \lambda\mathbf{c}\,.\,\mathbf{entry}\,\lambda\mathbf{e}\,.\,\mathcal{C}[\mathbf{C}]\,\mathbf{r[e/I_1]\,(exit\ c)}$$

$$\mathcal{E}[\mathbf{I}]\,\mathbf{r\,k} = \mathbf{(r\,I = unbound)} \rightarrow \mathbf{err},$$
$$\mathbf{isnoteval(r\,I)} \rightarrow \mathbf{eval(r\,I)\,k, k(r\,I)}$$

where, for example, ALGOL 60 call by value corresponds to

$$\begin{aligned} \mathbf{call\ p\ c\ E_2\ r} &= \mathcal{E}[\mathbf{E_2}]\,\mathbf{r;p\,c} \\ \mathbf{entry\ k} &= \mathbf{deref;ref;k} \\ \mathbf{exit\ c} &= \mathbf{c} \end{aligned}$$

whereas ALGOL 60 call by name corresponds to:

$$\begin{aligned} \mathbf{call\ p\ c\ E_2\ r} &= \mathbf{p\,c;}\mathcal{E}[\mathbf{E_2}]\,\mathbf{r} \\ \mathbf{entry\ k} &= \mathbf{k} \\ \mathbf{exit\ c} &= \mathbf{c} \\ \mathbf{eval\ e\ k} &= \mathbf{(e\,k)} \end{aligned}$$

Writing the semantics like this shows that many possibilities exist for manufacturing new kinds of procedures, by combining different calling and parameter passing mechanisms. For example, we could combine a call by closure calling mechanism with a call by value like parameter passing mechanism to get a system in which formal parameters denoted references to the closures of actual parameters. To do this we would take:

$$\begin{aligned} \mathbf{call\ p\ c\ E_2\ r} &= \mathbf{p\,c\,(}\mathcal{E}[\mathbf{E_2}]\,\mathbf{r)} \\ \mathbf{entry\ k} &= \mathbf{ref\ k} \end{aligned}$$

Finally, notice that everything we have said about procedures applies analogously to functions.

8.7. Procedure and function denoting expressions (abstractions)

In ALGOL 60 and PASCAL, one can pass a procedure (or function) as an actual parameter, but the only way of doing this is to write the procedure (or function) name directly. In other languages there are expressions other than identifiers, called *abstractions,* which evaluate to procedure (or function) values. For example, we might add to SMALL expressions **pr I;C** and **fn I;E** with semantics:

$$\mathcal{E}[\![\mathbf{pr}\ I;C]\!]\,r\,k = k(\lambda c\,e\,.\,\mathcal{C}[\![C]\!]\,r[e/I]\,c)$$
$$\mathcal{E}[\![\mathbf{fn}\ I;E]\!]\,r\,k = k(\lambda k'\,e\,.\,\mathcal{E}[\![E]\!]\,r[e/I]\,k')$$

Notice that with these constructs we can dispense with separate procedure and function declarations since **proc** $I(I_1);C$ is exactly equivalent to **const** $I=$ **pr** $I_1;C$ and **fun** $I(I_1);E$ is exactly equivalent to **const** $I =$ **fn** $I_1;E$. For example:

$$\begin{aligned} &\mathcal{D}[\![\mathbf{const}\ I=\mathbf{pr}\ I_1;C]\!]\,r\,u \\ &\quad = \mathcal{E}[\![\mathbf{pr}\ I_1;C]\!]\,r\,\lambda e\,.\,u(e/I) \\ &\quad = (\lambda e\,.\,u(e/I))\,\lambda c\,e\,.\,\mathcal{C}[\![C]\!]\,r[e/I_1]\,c \\ &\quad = u(\lambda c\,e\,.\,\mathcal{C}[\![C]\!]\,r[e/I_1]\,c/I) \\ &\quad = \mathcal{D}[\![\mathbf{proc}\ I(I_1);C]\!]\,r\,u \end{aligned}$$

Because the procedure (or function) denoted by **pr I;C** (or **fn I;E**) has no name these expressions are sometimes called *anonymous* procedures (or functions). Just as ordinary procedures (or functions) can have a variety of calling, parameter passing and identifier binding mechanisms, so can abstractions. For example, abstractions with call by value and dynamic binding would have semantics:

$$\mathcal{E}[\![\mathbf{pr}\ I;C]\!]\,r\,k = k(\lambda r'c\,.\,deref;ref\,\lambda\iota\,.\,\mathcal{C}[\![C]\!]\,r'[\iota/I]\,c)$$

In LISP, **(QUOTE (LAMBDA (X) E))** is dynamically bound, whereas **(FUNCTION (LAMBDA (X) E))** is statically bound (the latter is thus more analogous to **fn X;E** than the former).

8.8. Declaration binding mechanisms

A command of the form **begin var I = E;C end** is similar in effect to **(pr I;C)(E)**, where the parameter **I** is called by value. Both evaluate **C** in an environment in which **I** 'locally' denotes a reference to **E**'s R-value. Thus variable declarations are related to call by value. In fact, to any parameter passing mechanism, there corresponds a kind of declaration; for example, to abstractions **pr I;C** with semantics

$$\mathcal{E}[\![\mathbf{pr}\ I;C]\!]\,r\,k = k(\lambda c\,.\,entry\,\lambda e\,.\,\mathcal{C}[\![C]\!]\,r[e/I]\,c)$$

there correspond declarations **dec I = E** with semantics

$$\mathbf{D[dec\ I = E]\ r\ u = E[E]\ r;entry\ \lambda e\ .\ u(e/I)}$$

Thus **var I = E** corresponds to procedures with

$$\mathbf{entry\ k = deref;ref;k}$$

i.e. to call by value, whereas **const I = E** corresponds to procedures with

$$\mathbf{entry\ k = deref;k}$$

Procedures of this sort can be found lurking in ALGOL 68.
This semantic correspondence between declarations and parameter passing is often obscured in programming languages. For example, declarations might exist without there being any way of defining procedures with the corresponding parameter passing mechanism (or vice versa). PASCAL has been criticised on these grounds [Tennent] and the same criticisms can be applied to SMALL as follows: although there are constant declarations **const I = E,** there is no corresponding parameter passing method. Thus in SMALL (and PASCAL) there is no way of declaring a procedure **P** so that

begin const I = E;C end

is equivalent to **P(E)**.

9. Data Structures

In this chapter we discuss four kinds of data structures: references (pointers), arrays, records and files. References have a single component, arrays and records have several components (the number being determined when the structure is declared) and files have a dynamically varying number of components. The components of arrays are accessed with a subscript (e.g. **A[3]**) whereas the components of records are accessed with a name (e.g. **R.three**). The components of files are accessed by moving a 'window' up and down the file.

These four data structures are precisely those that are found in PASCAL. We illustrate the main ideas (but *not* all the details) in the context of SMALL (indicating here and there how things differ in PASCAL).

9.1. References

A reference to a value is just a location holding it. Suppose **ref I = E** is a declaration which binds **I** to a reference to **E**'s value, and **cont E** is an expression whose value is the *contents* of the reference denoted by **E**; then:

$$\mathbf{D}[\![\mathbf{ref\ I = E}]\!]\,\mathbf{r\,u} = \mathbf{E}[\![\mathbf{E}]\!]\,\mathbf{r;ref}\,\lambda\iota\,.\,\mathbf{u}(\iota/\mathbf{I})$$
$$\mathbf{E}[\![\mathbf{cont\ E}]\!]\,\mathbf{r\,k} = \mathbf{E}[\![\mathbf{E}]\!]\,\mathbf{r;Loc?;cont;k}$$

Thus if **E**'s value is a location ι then **ref I = E** binds **I** to another location containing ι. This differs from **var I = E,** which would bind **I** to a location containing ι's contents. To illustrate **cont E**, suppose identifiers $\mathbf{I}_1$ and $\mathbf{I}_2$ denote locations ι_1 and ι_2 respectively; then:

$$\begin{aligned}
&\mathbf{C}[\![\mathbf{cont\ I_1 := cont\ I_2}]\!]\,\mathbf{r\,c}\\
&\quad = \mathbf{E}[\![\mathbf{cont\ I_1}]\!]\,\mathbf{r;Loc?}\\
&\qquad\quad \lambda\iota\,.\,\mathbf{R}[\![\mathbf{cont\ I_2}]\!]\,\mathbf{r;update}\,\iota\,\mathbf{c}\\
&\quad = \mathbf{E}[\![\mathbf{I_1}]\!]\,\mathbf{r;Loc?;cont;Loc?}\\
&\qquad\quad \lambda\iota\,.\,\mathbf{E}[\![\mathbf{cont\ I_2}]\!]\,\mathbf{r;deref;Rv?;update}\,\iota\,\mathbf{c}\\
&\quad = \mathbf{E}[\![\mathbf{I_1}]\!]\,\mathbf{r;Loc?;cont;Loc?}\\
&\qquad\quad \lambda\iota\,.\,\mathbf{E}[\![\mathbf{I_2}]\!]\,\mathbf{r;Loc?;cont;deref;Rv?;update}\,\iota\,\mathbf{c}
\end{aligned}$$

Thus we update the location which is the contents of ι_1 with the dereferenced contents of ι_2—i.e. the contents of the contents of ι_2.

9.2. Arrays

An array is a data structure whose components are accessed with *subscripts*. References are like the special case of arrays with just one component. To declare an array **A** with components **A[1]**, **A[2]**, ..., **A[n]** we shall use the declaration **array A[1;n]**. Normally each component of an array is a variable which is initially unassigned; however constant arrays are possible. In the former case, array components can be changed by assignment; in the latter, this would cause an error. We shall just deal with arrays of variables subscripted by integers (as in ALGOL 60); other possibilities such as constant arrays, or arrays subscripted by other values, can be handled in an analogous way.

Thus, in general, a declaration **array** $\mathbf{I[E_1;E_2]}$ binds **I** to an array value, and this value contains:

(i) The lower bound, $\mathbf{n}_1$ say, specified by $\mathbf{E}_1$.
(ii) The upper bound, $\mathbf{n}_2$ say, specified by $\mathbf{E}_2$:
(iii) The $\mathbf{n}_2\text{-}\mathbf{n}_1+\mathbf{1}$ locations comprising the array.

A suitable domain **Array** of array values is thus:

$$\mathbf{Array} = \mathbf{Num} \times \mathbf{Num} \times \mathbf{Loc}^*$$

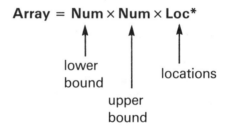

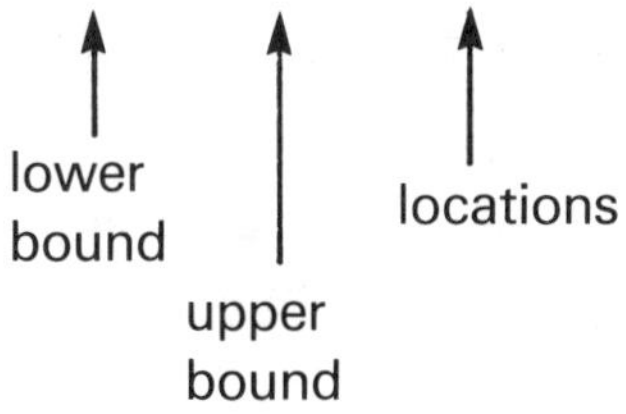

Each time **array** $\mathbf{I[E_1;E_2]}$ is evaluated, $\mathbf{E}_1$ will be evaluated to get $\mathbf{n}_1$; $\mathbf{E}_2$ will be evaluated to get $\mathbf{n}_2$, and then new locations $\mathbf{l}_1$, $\mathbf{l}_2$, ..., $\mathbf{l}_n$ (where $\mathbf{n} = \mathbf{n}_2\text{-}\mathbf{n}_1 + \mathbf{1}$) will be obtained and the array value $(\mathbf{n}_1, \mathbf{n}_2, \mathbf{l}_1 . \mathbf{l}_2 . \ldots . \mathbf{l}_n)$ bound to **I**. To access array components we use expressions of the form $\mathbf{E_1[E_2]}$; the value of $\mathbf{E}_1$ must be an array value and the value of $\mathbf{E}_2$ an integer between the lower and upper bounds. $\mathbf{E_1[E_2]}$ then denotes the appropriate location. To simplify the semantic clauses for array declaration and accessing, it helps to first define some functions.

9.2.1. **news**

Informal description

news:Num→Store→[[Loc* × Store] + {error}]

$$\mathbf{news\ ns} = \begin{cases} (\iota_1 \ldots \iota_n, & \text{if } \mathbf{s} \text{ has unused} \\ \quad \mathbf{s[unassigned,\ldots,unassigned}/\iota_1,\ldots,\iota_n]) & \text{locations } \iota_1,\ldots,\iota_n \\ \mathbf{error} & \text{otherwise} \end{cases}$$

Thus **news n s** gets **n** new locations from **s** and returns them, together with a store in which they each have contents **unassigned**.

Formal description

$$\begin{aligned} \mathbf{news} = \lambda \mathbf{n\,s}.\ & (\mathbf{n}=0)\rightarrow((\,),\mathbf{s}), \\ & ((\mathbf{news}\,(\mathbf{n}\text{-}1) = (\iota^*,\mathbf{s}'))\rightarrow \\ & \ ((\mathbf{new\ s}' = \iota)\rightarrow(\iota\,.\,\iota^*,\mathbf{s}'[\mathbf{unassigned}/\iota]),\mathbf{error}), \\ & \ \mathbf{error}) \end{aligned}$$

9.2.2. **newarray**

Informal description

newarray:[Num × Num]→Ec→Cc

newarray $(\mathbf{n}_1,\mathbf{n}_2)$ **k s** = **k e s′** where **e** is the array value $(\mathbf{n}_1,\mathbf{n}_2,\iota_1 \ldots \iota_n)$ $(\mathbf{n}=\mathbf{n}_2\text{-}\mathbf{n}_1+1)$ and $\mathbf{s}' = \mathbf{s[unassigned,\ldots,unassigned}/\iota_1,\ldots,\iota_n]$. Thus **newarray** $(\mathbf{n}_1,\mathbf{n}_2)$ **k** sends a new array value on to **k**, together with a modified store.

Formal description

$$\begin{aligned} \mathbf{newarray} = \lambda(\mathbf{n}_1,\mathbf{n}_2)\,\mathbf{k\,s}.\ & \\ & (\mathbf{n}_1>\mathbf{n}_2)\rightarrow\mathbf{error}, \\ & (\mathbf{news}\,(\mathbf{n}_2\text{-}\mathbf{n}_1+1)\,\mathbf{s}=(\iota^*,\mathbf{s}'))\rightarrow\mathbf{k}(\mathbf{n}_1,\mathbf{n}_2,\iota^*)\,\mathbf{s}',\mathbf{error} \end{aligned}$$

9.2.3. **subscript**

Informal description

subscript:Array→Ec→Ec

$$\textbf{subscript a k e} = \begin{cases} \textbf{k}\,\iota & \text{if } \iota \text{ is the } \textbf{e}\text{th component of array } \textbf{a} \\ \textbf{err} & \text{otherwise} \end{cases}$$

subscript a k e checks that **e** is a number between the bounds of **a**, and if so, sends to **k** the appropriate location.

Formal description

$$\textbf{subscript} = \lambda(\textbf{n}_1,\textbf{n}_2,\iota^*)\,\textbf{k e}\,.\ \textbf{isNum e}\rightarrow(\textbf{between}\,(\textbf{n}_1,\textbf{n}_2)\,\textbf{e}\rightarrow\textbf{k}(\textbf{el}\,(\textbf{e-n}_1+1)\iota^*),\textbf{err}),\textbf{err}$$

where **between** $(\mathbf{n}_1,\mathbf{n}_2)$ **e** is **true** if $\mathbf{n}_1$ is less than or equal to $\mathbf{n}_2$ and **e** is between them, and **false** otherwise.

We can now write the semantics of array declarations and accesses:

$$\mathbf{D}[\![\textbf{array I}[\textbf{E}_1;\textbf{E}_2]]\!]\,\textbf{r u}$$
$$= \mathbf{R}[\![\textbf{E}_1]\!]\,\textbf{r;Num?}$$
$$\lambda\textbf{n}_1\,.\,\mathbf{R}[\![\textbf{E}_2]\!]\,\textbf{r;Num?}\,\lambda\textbf{n}_2\,.\,\textbf{newarray}\,(\textbf{n}_1,\textbf{n}_2)\,\lambda\textbf{e}\,.\,\textbf{u(e/I)}$$

$$\mathbf{E}[\![\textbf{E}_1[\textbf{E}_2]]\!]\,\textbf{r k}$$
$$= \mathbf{E}[\![\textbf{E}_1]\!]\,\textbf{r;Array?}\,\lambda\textbf{e}\,.\,\mathbf{R}[\![\textbf{E}_2]\!]\,\textbf{r;Num?;subscript e k}$$

In PASCAL, array bounds are fixed at compile time, so in **array** $\mathbf{I}[\mathbf{E}_1;\mathbf{E}_2]$, the bounds expressions $\mathbf{E}_1$ and $\mathbf{E}_2$ must be evaluable then.

9.3. Records

A record is a data structure with a fixed number of named components or *fields*. We shall use **record** $\mathbf{I}(\mathbf{I}_1,\ldots,\mathbf{I}_n)$ to declare a record named **I** with fields named $\mathbf{I}_1,\ldots,\mathbf{I}_n$. As with arrays we shall assume each component is a location which can be assigned to. To access component **I** of a record denoted by **E**, we use the expression **E . I**. To illustrate records, here is a declaration of a record named **family** with field names **father, mother, son, daughter**:

record family (father, mother, son, daughter)

To initialize this we could do:

```
family . father   := "Phil";
family . mother   := "Liz";
family . son      := "Charlie";
family . daughter := "Annie";
```

(assuming quotations such as "**Phil**" are valid expressions).

In PASCAL there is a command **with E do C**, which when evaluated first evaluates **E** and checks its value is a record; then evaluates **C** in an environment in which each field name of this record is bound to the corresponding field. The initialization of **family** could thus be achieved more succinctly by:

with family do father := "Phil";
mother := "Liz";
son := "Charlie";
daughter := "Annie"

Notice that **E . I** and **with E do C** are similar; both cause the evaluation of a construct—**I** in the case of **E . I**, and **C** in the case of **with E do C**—in an environment in which the field names of the record denoted by **E** denote the corresponding fields. Thus both **E . I** and **with E do C** are kinds of blocks—**E** acts like a declaration (of field names) and **I** (in the case of **E . I**) or **C** (in the case of **with E do C**) is the body. This observation suggests two things:

(i) That **E . I** be generalized to $\mathbf{E_1 . E_2}$—i.e. the 'body' of the 'block' be allowed to be a full expression. This would then allow things like **E . (if...then mother else father)**.

(ii) That a syntax should be chosen which expresses the similarity between **E . I** and **with E do C**. For example *either* **E . I** and **E . C** *or* **with E do I** and **with E do C**.

For the semantics of records we must define a domain **Record** of record values. Since records specify a location for each field name, an appropriate domain is:

$$\mathbf{Record} = \mathbf{Ide} \rightarrow [\mathbf{Dv} + \{\mathbf{unbound}\}] = \mathbf{Env}$$

By using **Dv** here rather than just **Loc**, we allow for the possibility (not discussed above) that record fields can be other things than locations. If $\mathbf{r} \varepsilon \mathbf{Record}$ then $\mathbf{r\ I = unbound}$ means **I** is not a field name of **E**.

The semantics of the various constructs is now routine:

$$\mathbf{D[record\ I(I_1,\ldots,I_n)]\ r\ u\ s}$$
$$= (\mathbf{news\ n\ s} = (\iota_1 \ldots . \iota_n, s')) \rightarrow \mathbf{u}((\iota_1,\ldots,\iota_n/\mathbf{I}_1,\ldots,\mathbf{I}_n)/\mathbf{I})\ s', \mathbf{error}$$

$\mathcal{E}[\![E_1 . E_2]\!]\, r\, k$
$= \mathcal{E}[\![E_1]\!]\, r;\text{Record?}\, \lambda r' . \mathcal{E}[\![E_2]\!]\, r[r']\, k$

$\mathcal{C}[\![\textbf{with}\ E\ \textbf{do}\ C]\!]\, r\, c$
$= \mathcal{E}[\![E]\!]\, r;\text{Record?}\, \lambda r' . \mathcal{C}[\![C]\!]\, r[r']\, c$

Notice how the semantics brings out the similarity between $E_1 . E_2$ and **with E do C**, and the similarity between these and **begin D;C end**. Notice also that a declaration **record** $I(I_1,\ldots,I_n)$ somewhat resembles a procedure declaration **proc** $I(I_1,\ldots,I_n)$;C but without the body **C**. In SL5 [Hanson], procedures can be called but 'not entered' (the formal parameters are bound to actual parameters, but the body is not executed), and one use of this is to enable procedures to double up as records. One can, in effect, declare **proc** $I(I_1,\ldots,I_n)$ (no body) and then a 'call' $I(E_1,\ldots,E_n)$ creates an entity which can be used like a record—the formal parameters being the field names and the actual parameters the contents of the fields.

9.4. Data structure valued expressions

Instead of having *declarations* **ref** I = E, **array** $I[E_1;E_2]$ and **record** $I(I_1,\ldots,I_n)$, one could have *expressions* **ref** E, **array** $[E_1;E_2]$ and **record** $(I_1,\ldots,I_n)$, so that:

ref I = E is equivalent to **const** I = **ref** E
array $I[E_1;E_2]$ is equivalent to **const** I = **array** $[E_1;E_2]$
record $I(I_1,\ldots,I_n)$ is equivalent to **const** I = **record** $(I_1,\ldots,I_n)$

Thus the expressions are related to the declarations as **pr** I_1;C is related to **proc** $I(I_1)$;C (see 8.7.). The semantics of data structure valued expressions is straightforward:

$\mathcal{E}[\![\textbf{ref}\ E]\!]\, r\, k = \mathcal{E}[\![E]\!]\, r;\text{ref}\, k$

$\mathcal{E}[\![\textbf{array}\ [E_1;E_2]]\!]\, r\, k =$
$\mathcal{R}[\![E_1]\!]\, r;\text{Num?}\, \lambda n_1 . \mathcal{R}[\![E_2]\!]\, r;\text{Num?}\, \lambda n_2 . \text{newarray}(n_1,n_2)\, k$

$\mathcal{E}[\![\textbf{record}\ (I_1,\ldots,I_n)]\!]\, r\, k =$
$\lambda s . (\text{news}\ n\ s = (\iota_1 . \ldots . \iota_n,s')) \rightarrow k(\iota_1,\ldots,\iota_n/I_1,\ldots,I_n)\, s',\text{error}$

Using expressions like these has the advantage that it makes apparent that when we declare a data structure in SMALL we are really declaring a *constant* with *variable components*.

Data structure variables (which are what occur in PASCAL) would be declared by:

var I = **ref** E
var I = **array** [E_1;E_2]
var I = **record** (I_1,...,I_n)

To ensure that such variables work we must dereference them when accessing components of their contents. For example, instead of

$$\mathbf{E}[E_1 \,.\, E_2]\, r\, k = \mathbf{E}[E_1]\, r; Record?\, \lambda r' \,.\, \mathbf{E}[E_2]\, r[r']\, k$$

we must have:

$$\mathbf{E}[E_1 \,.\, E_2]\, r\, k = \mathbf{R}[E_1]\, r; Record?\, \lambda r' \,.\, \mathbf{E}[E_2]\, r[r']\, k$$

↑ N.B.

The changes to the other clauses are analogous—i.e. replacement of some occurrences of **E** by **R**. However notice that confusion can arise between *variables* (locations created using **var I** = **E**) and *references* (locations created using **ref E**). For example, in our semantics of **var I** = **E**, **E**'s value is dereferenced and so both **var x** = **1** and **var x** = **ref 1** would bind **x** to a location containing **1**. One needs to get clear—and this is really a language design problem—whether variables and references are the same or different; and hence, for example, whether **R** should only dereference locations created by variable declarations, or all locations, including those obtained by evaluting **ref E**. In short, one must decide which dereferencing coercions are to be automatic.

9.5. Files

In this section we describe how to model PASCAL-like file structures. Such files are sequences of values such that:

(i) The number of components can vary dynamically—unlike arrays it is not fixed when the structure is created.
(ii) Component values are accessed via a 'window' which can be moved up and down the file and whose position defines the effect of 'reading' and 'writing' operations.
(iii) Associated with each file is a buffer variable which provides the

channel through which values are read or written.

We shall use **file** $\mathbf{I}_1$ **withbuffer** $\mathbf{I}_2$ to declare a file named $\mathbf{I}_1$ with buffer variable denoted by $\mathbf{I}_2$. The effect of the declaration is to make both $\mathbf{I}_1$ and $\mathbf{I}_2$ denote new locations, ι_1 and ι_2 say, where ι_1 holds an 'empty' file value and ι_2 holds **unassigned**. We call ι_1 the *file variable* and ι_2 the *buffer variable*.

If **E** is an expression whose value is a file variable then the meaning of the expression **eof E**, and of commands **reset E**, **rewrite E**, **get E** and **put E** are informally as follows:

eof E:

If the window is beyond the end of the file then **eof E** evaluates to **true**; if the window is within the file then it evaluates to **false**.

reset E:

The window is reset to the beginning of the file and the first component is assigned to the buffer variable (if the file is empty, the buffer is assigned **unassigned**).

rewrite E:

The file is emptied, the window is reset to the beginning and the buffer variable is assigned **unassigned**.

get E:

The window is advanced to the next component and the value of this component is assigned to the buffer variable. If the window is not within the file, an error occurs; if it is at the last element, **unassigned** is assigned to the buffer variable.

put E:

The contents of the buffer variable is appended to the file. The window must be at the first free space in the file; otherwise an error will occur.

In PASCAL, instead of having these constructs one has equivalent 'pre-declared' functions and procedures. To model this, one just modifies the semantic clause for $\mathbf{P}$ by replacing the empty environment **()** by one containing the desired initial bindings (see 6.2.3.1.).

The domain of *file values* must model:

(i) The sequence of component values (we shall assume these are R-values).
(ii) The position of the window.
(iii) The buffer variable.

We thus define:

$$\mathbf{File} = \mathbf{Rv}^* \times \mathbf{Num} \times \mathbf{Loc}$$

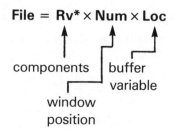

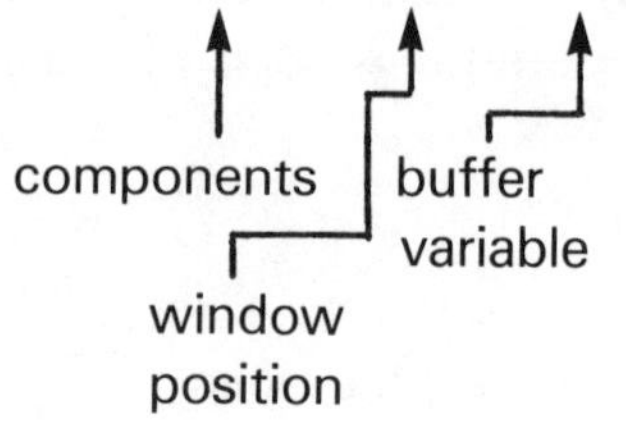

The semantics of file declarations is then:

$$\mathcal{D}[\![\mathbf{file}\ \mathrm{I}_1\ \mathbf{withbuffer}\ \mathrm{I}_2]\!]\,\mathbf{r\,u\,s} =$$
$$(\mathbf{news\,2\,s}=(\iota_1\,.\,\iota_2,\mathbf{s}'))\rightarrow\mathbf{u}(\iota_1,\iota_2/\mathrm{I}_1,\mathrm{I}_2)(\mathbf{s}'[((\ ),1,\iota_2)/\iota_1]),\mathbf{error}$$

We get two new locations ι_1 and ι_2 and then pass the binding $\iota_1,\iota_2/\mathrm{I}_1,\mathrm{I}_2$, together with a store in which ι_1 holds the empty file $((\ ),1,\iota_2)$ and ι_2 holds **unassigned**, to the rest of the program **u** (see 9.2.1. for details of **news**).

The semantics of **eof E** is:

$$\mathcal{E}[\![\mathbf{eof}\ \mathrm{E}]\!]\,\mathbf{r\,k} =$$
$$\mathcal{E}[\![\mathrm{E}]\!]\,\mathbf{r};\mathbf{Loc?}\,\lambda\iota\,\mathbf{s}\,.\,(\mathbf{s}\,\iota=(\mathbf{e}^*,\mathbf{n},\iota'))\rightarrow\mathbf{k}(\mathbf{n}>\mathbf{length}\ \mathbf{e}^*)\,\mathbf{s},\mathbf{error}$$

We evaluate **E**, test that its value is a location holding a file value $(\mathbf{e}^*,\mathbf{n},\iota')$, and then send the result of the test $\mathbf{n}>\mathbf{length}\ \mathbf{e}^*$ to the rest of the program **k**.

Semantic clauses for the other constructs can easily be written in a similar way to this, but unless one is careful, messy details rapidly obscure what is going on. To simplify the semantics it is convenient to define the domain:

$$\mathbf{Filestate} = \mathbf{Rv}^* \times \mathbf{Num} \times [\mathbf{Rv} + \{\mathbf{unassigned}\}]$$

A member $(\mathbf{e}^*,\mathbf{n},\mathbf{e})$ of **Filestate** represents the 'state' of a file whose components are **e***, whose window position is **n** and whose buffer variable holds **e**. The effects of **reset E**, **rewrite E**, **get E** and **put E** can now be described with the 'state' transformations **resetf**, **rewritef**, **getf** and **putf**, which are the functions of type **Filestate→[Filestate + {error}]** defined by:

resetf(e*,n,e) = null e*→(e*,1,unassigned) , (e*,1,el 1 e*)

rewritef(e*,n,e) = (( ),1,unassigned)

getf(e*,n,e) = (n>length e*)→error,
(n = length e*)→(e*,n + 1,unassigned),
(n<length e*)→(e*,n + 1,el (n + 1) e*)

putf(e*,n,e) = (n = length e* + 1)→(e* . e,n + 1,unassigned),
error

These functions constitute a direct semantics of the file operations. To 'interface' them to a continuation semantics we define a function:

do:[Filestate→[Filestate + {error}]]→Cc→Ec

where informally

do f c e s = c s′ where **s′** is a store derived from **s** by doing the file state transformation **f** on the file in the file variable **e**.

do is analogous to the function **mkconfun** discussed in 5.7. The formal description of it is rather messy:

```
do f c e s = isLoc e→
              ((s e = (e*,n,ı))→
               ((s ı = e′)→
                ((f(e*,n,e′) = (e*′,n′,e″))→
                 c(s[(e*′,n′,ı),e″/e,ı]),
                 error),
                error),
               error),
              error
```

If **e** is a file variable whose contents in **s** is the file **(e*,n,ı)**, and if the buffer variable **ı** has contents **e′**, and if **f(e*,n,e′) = (e*′,n′,e″)** then the file variable **e** is updated with the new file value **(e*′,n′,ı)** and the buffer variable **ı** is updated with **e**″, and the resulting store passed to **c**.

We can now write the remaining semantic clauses very simply:

C[reset E] r c = **E[E] r;do resetf c**
C[rewrite E] r c = **E[E] r;do rewritef c**
C[get E] r c = **E[E] r;do getf c**
C[put E] r c = **E[E] r;do putf c**

The 'real meaning' is clearly expressed in the definitions of **resetf**, **rewritef**, **getf** and **putf**, whilst all the messiness is factored out into the definition of **do**.

10. Iteration constructs

In SMALL, the only iteration construct is **while E do C**. In this chapter we look briefly at three others: **repeat C until E**, **loop C then** I_1:C_1;...;I_n:C_n **end** together with **event I**, and for-statements **for I: = F do C**. The first two of these are minor variations on constructs we have already met; for-statements are a bit more tricky since we have to devise denotations for 'for-lists' **F**.

10.1. repeat C until E

This construct is found in PASCAL and has semantics:

$$\mathcal{C}[\textbf{repeat C until E}]\,r\,c =$$
$$\mathcal{C}[C]\,r;\mathcal{R}[E]\,r;Bool?;cond(c,\mathcal{C}[\textbf{repeat C until E}]\,r\,c)$$

We evaluate **C** then evaluate **E**; if **E**'s value is **false** then we evaluate **repeat C until E** again, but if it is **true,** we proceed to the rest of the program **c**.

10.2. Event loops

The construct described in this section has been advocated as good for 'structured programming' [Knuth 74]. It is very similar to the escapes from commands described in 7.1.1. The idea is that one has a command **loop C then** I_1:C_1,...,I_n:C_n **end** which traps escapes invoked by evaluating the command **event I**. The body **C** of the event loop is repeatedly evaluated until an event **event** I_i is encountered, whereupon the postlude C_i is done and control proceeds to the rest of the program. Thus:

$$\mathcal{C}[\textbf{loop C then } I_1{:}C_1,\ldots,I_nC_n \textbf{ end}]\,r\,c =$$
$$\mathcal{C}[C]\,r[\mathcal{C}[C_1]\,r\,c,\ldots,\mathcal{C}[C_n]\,r\,c/I_1,\ldots,I_n];$$
$$\mathcal{C}[\textbf{loopC then } I_1{:}C_1,\ldots,I_n{:}C_n \textbf{ end}]\,r\,c$$

(notice the recursion)

$$\mathcal{C}[\textbf{event I}]\,r\,c = \mathcal{E}[I]\,r;Cc?\ \lambda c'.\,c'$$

(this is just like the clause for **escapeto I** and **goto I**).

10.3. For-statements

We shall discuss the "for-statements" of ALGOL 60—a special case of these is found in PASCAL. ALGOL 60 style for-statements are commands of the form **for I: = F do C** where **F** is a member of the syntactic domain **For** of *for-lists* defined by:

$$\mathbf{F} ::= \mathbf{E} \mid \mathbf{E}_1 \textbf{ while } \mathbf{E}_2 \mid \mathbf{E}_1 \textbf{ step } \mathbf{E}_2 \textbf{ until } \mathbf{E}_3 \mid \mathbf{F}_1, \mathbf{F}_2$$

For each particular for-list it is straightforward to write a semantic clause for the corresponding for-statement. For example, it is easy to define

$$\mathcal{C}[\textbf{for I} := \mathbf{E}_1 \textbf{ while } \mathbf{E}_2 \textbf{ do C}]$$

or $\mathcal{C}[\textbf{for I} := \mathbf{E}_1 \textbf{ step } \mathbf{E}_2 \textbf{ until } \mathbf{E}_3 \textbf{ do C}]$

or even $\mathcal{C}[\textbf{for I} := \mathbf{E}_1 \textbf{ while } \mathbf{E}_2, \mathbf{E}_3 \textbf{ step } \mathbf{E}_4 \textbf{ until } \mathbf{E}_5 \textbf{ do C}]$

However, since there are *infinitely* many different for-lists, it is necessary (as well as aesthetically pleasing) to have a *single* clause for $\mathcal{C}$[**for I: = F do C**] and then a separate clause for each of the four different kinds of for-list **F**.

Thus we must devise denotations $\mathcal{F}$[**F**] for for-lists **F** and then:

(i) Write $\mathcal{C}$[**for I: = F do C**] in terms of $\mathcal{F}$[**F**]
(ii) Write semantic clauses for $\mathcal{F}$[**F**].

Before formalizing the semantics we must be clear about the meaning we are going to express—there have been several incompatible interpretations of the original descriptions of ALGOL 60 for-statements. For us the effect of **for I: = F do C** is:

(i) If **I** denotes a location **ι** and if **F** specifies a sequence of values $\mathbf{e}_1, \ldots, \mathbf{e}_n$ then **C** is executed **n** times with **ι** successively containing these values.
(ii) On exiting the for-statement the final contents of **ι** is whatever the last iteration of **C** left in it.

Thus, roughly speaking, the effect of **for I: = F do C** is equivalent to $\mathbf{I} := \mathbf{e}_1; \mathbf{C}; \mathbf{I} := \mathbf{e}_2; \mathbf{C}; \ldots; \mathbf{I} := \mathbf{e}_n; \mathbf{C}$ (this does not really make sense, as the $\mathbf{e}_i$'s are not expressions, but perhaps it conveys the idea).

The way we shall model this is for $\mathcal{C}$[**for I: = F do C**] to pass to $\mathcal{F}$[**F**] the procedure value $\mathbf{p} = \lambda \mathbf{c} \,.\, \textbf{update } \iota; \mathcal{C}[\mathbf{C}]\ \mathbf{r}\ \mathbf{c}$, which when applied to a value, stores it in ι and then does **C**. **F**[**F**] can then apply **p** to the arguments specified by **F** (i.e. to $e_1,\ldots,e_n$ of (i) above). For example, in **for I: = 1,2,3 do C**, we would apply **p** successively to **1,2,3**.

A semantics based on this idea is as follows:

Semantic function:

$$\mathbf{F}:\mathbf{For}\rightarrow\mathbf{Env}\rightarrow\mathbf{Proc}\rightarrow\mathbf{Cc}\rightarrow\mathbf{Cc}$$

Then **F[F] r p c** applies **p** successively to values generated by **F** and then passes control to the rest of the program **c**.

Semantic clauses:

$$\mathbf{C}[\textbf{for I:} = \textbf{F do C}]\,\mathbf{r}\,\mathbf{c} =$$
$$\mathbf{E}[\mathbf{I}]\,\mathbf{r};\mathbf{Loc?}\,\lambda\iota\,.\,\mathbf{F}[\mathbf{F}]\,\mathbf{r}\,(\lambda\mathbf{c}'\,.\,\mathbf{update}\,\iota;\mathbf{C}[\mathbf{C}]\,\mathbf{r}\,\mathbf{c}')\,\mathbf{c}$$

Thus **I** is evaluated, its value is checked to ensure it is a location ι, and then **F**[**F**] **r p c** is done, where $\mathbf{p} = \lambda\mathbf{c}'\,.\,\mathbf{update}\,\iota;\mathbf{C}[\mathbf{C}]\,\mathbf{r}\,\mathbf{c}'$.

We now give the semantic clauses for **F**[**F**]. Recall that:

$$\mathbf{F} ::= \mathbf{E} \mid \mathbf{E}_1\ \textbf{while}\ \mathbf{E}_2 \mid \mathbf{E}_1\ \textbf{step}\ \mathbf{E}_2\ \textbf{until}\ \mathbf{E}_3 \mid \mathbf{F}_1,\mathbf{F}_2$$

then:

$$\mathbf{F}[\mathbf{E}]\,\mathbf{r}\,\mathbf{p}\,\mathbf{c} = \mathbf{R}[\mathbf{E}]\,\mathbf{r};\mathbf{p}\,\mathbf{c}$$

Thus the for-list **E**—a simple expression—just 'calls' **p** with 'actual parameter value' the R-value of **E**.

$$\mathbf{F}[\mathbf{E}_1\ \textbf{while}\ \mathbf{E}_2]\,\mathbf{r}\,\mathbf{p}\,\mathbf{c} =$$
$$\mathbf{R}[\mathbf{E}_1]\,\mathbf{r}\,\lambda\mathbf{e}\,.\,\mathbf{R}[\mathbf{E}_2]\,\mathbf{r};\mathbf{Bool?cond}(\mathbf{p}(\mathbf{F}[\mathbf{E}_1\ \textbf{while}\ \mathbf{E}_2]\,\mathbf{r}\,\mathbf{p}\,\mathbf{c})\mathbf{e},\mathbf{c})$$

Thus $\mathbf{E}_1$ is evaluated for its R-value **e**; then $\mathbf{E}_2$ is evaluated, and if it yields **true** then **p** is applied to **e** with 'return address' the beginning of $\mathbf{E}_1$ **while** $\mathbf{E}_2$. If $\mathbf{E}_2$ yields **false,** then control immediately passes to the rest of the program **c**.

$$\begin{aligned}
&\mathbf{F[E_1\ step\ E_2\ until\ E_3]\ r\ p\ c} = \\
&\quad \mathbf{R[E_1]\ r;Num?;step\ (R[E_2]\ r,R[E_3]\ r)\ p\ c} \\
&\mathbf{where} \\
&\quad \mathbf{step\ (w_1,w_2)\ p\ c\ n} = \\
&\qquad \mathbf{w_1;Num?\lambda n_1\ .\ w_2;Num?\ \lambda n_2\ .} \\
&\qquad\quad \mathbf{(n\text{-}n_2) \times (sign\ n_1) < 1 \rightarrow p(step\ (w_1,w_2)\ p\ c\ (n+n_1))n,c}
\end{aligned}$$

Here **step**:[**Closure** × **Closure**]→**Proc**→**Cc**→**Ec**, where **Closure** = **Ec**→**Cc** is the domain of closures discussed in 8.5.1. The details of the semantic clause for $\mathbf{E_1}$ **step** $\mathbf{E_2}$ **until** $\mathbf{E_3}$ are a bit intricate, and if the reader wishes to check that we have got things right he should first read 4.6.4.2. of the modified report on ALGOL 60 [Backus *et al.*]. The idea is that we evaluate $\mathbf{E_1}$ *once* and check that it produces a number **n**, which we then pass to **step** $\mathbf{(w_1,w_2)}$ **p c**, where $\mathbf{w_1}$ and $\mathbf{w_2}$ are the closures $\mathbf{R[E_2]\ r}$ and $\mathbf{R[E_3]\ r}$, respectively. Then 'each time around the loop', **step** evaluates $\mathbf{w_1}$ and $\mathbf{w_2}$ to get numbers $\mathbf{n_1}$ and $\mathbf{n_2}$; if we have not finished ($\mathbf{(n\text{-}n_2) \times (sign\ n_1)<1}$) then **p** is applied to **n** with a 'return address' consisting of **step** $\mathbf{(w_1,w_2)\ p\ c\ (n_1 + n)}$—i.e. we increment **n** by $\mathbf{n_1}$ and start again. When we have incremented **n** past $\mathbf{n_2}$, then control passes to the rest of the program **c**. If the reader wants to but cannot follow this, he is advised to evaluate **for I: = 1 step 1 until 2 do C**. The result should be the same as **for I: = 1,2 do C**, which we evaluate as a simple example shortly. First, the remaining semantic clause for for-lists $\mathbf{F_1,F_2}$

$$\mathbf{F[F_1,F_2]\ r\ p\ c = F[F_1]\ r\ p;F[F_2]\ r\ p;c}$$

Thus $\mathbf{F_1}$ repeatedly calls **p** until it is finished, and then $\mathbf{F_2}$ repeatedly calls **p**, and finally control passes to **c**.

Here is an example to illustrate how things work:

$$\begin{aligned}
&\mathbf{C[for\ I:=1,2\ do\ C]\ r\ c} \\
&\quad = \mathbf{E[I]\ r;Loc?\ \lambda\iota\ .\ F[1,2]\ r\ (\lambda c'\ .\ update\ \iota;C[C]\ r\ c')\ c}
\end{aligned}$$

Now $\mathbf{F[1,2]\ r\ p\ c}$

$$\begin{aligned}
&= \mathbf{F[1]\ r\ p;F[2]\ r\ p;c} \\
&= \mathbf{F[1]\ r\ p\ (F[2]\ r\ p\ c)} \\
&= \mathbf{R[1]\ r;p\ (R[2]\ r;p\ c)} \\
&= \mathbf{R[1]\ r\ (p(R[2]\ r\ (p\ c)))} \\
&= \mathbf{p\ (R[2]\ r\ (p\ c))\ 1} \\
&= \mathbf{p\ (p\ c\ 2)\ 1}
\end{aligned}$$

and if $\mathbf{p} = \lambda\mathbf{c}' . \mathbf{update}\ \iota;\mathcal{C}[\mathbf{C}]\ \mathbf{r}\ \mathbf{c}'$ then

$$\begin{aligned}
&\mathbf{p}\,(\mathbf{p}\,\mathbf{c}\,2)\,1\,\mathbf{s}\\
&\quad = \mathbf{update}\ \iota\,(\mathcal{C}[\mathbf{C}]\,\mathbf{r}\,(\mathbf{p}\,\mathbf{c}\,2))\,1\,\mathbf{s}\\
&\quad = \mathcal{C}[\mathbf{C}]\,\mathbf{r}\,(\mathbf{p}\,\mathbf{c}\,2)\,\mathbf{s}[1/\iota]\\
&\quad = \mathcal{C}[\mathbf{C}]\,\mathbf{r}\,(\mathbf{update}\ \iota\,(\mathcal{C}[\mathbf{C}]\,\mathbf{r}\,\mathbf{c})\,2)\,\mathbf{s}[1/\iota]\\
&\quad = \mathcal{C}[\mathbf{C}]\,\mathbf{r}\,(\lambda\mathbf{s}' . \mathcal{C}[\mathbf{C}]\,\mathbf{r}\,\mathbf{c}\,\mathbf{s}'[2/\iota])\,\mathbf{s}[1/\iota]
\end{aligned}$$

Thus

$$\begin{aligned}
&\mathcal{C}[\mathbf{for}\ \mathbf{I} := 1,2\ \mathbf{do}\ \mathbf{C}]\,\mathbf{r}\,\mathbf{c}\,\mathbf{s}\\
&\quad = \mathcal{E}[\mathbf{I}]\,\mathbf{r};\mathbf{Loc?}\,\lambda\iota . \mathcal{C}[\mathbf{C}]\,\mathbf{r}\,(\lambda\mathbf{s}' . \mathcal{C}[\mathbf{C}]\,\mathbf{r}\,\mathbf{c}\,(\mathbf{s}'[2/\iota]))\,(\mathbf{s}[1/\iota])
\end{aligned}$$

So **C** is first executed in the store $\mathbf{s}[1/\iota]$ to yield a new store $\mathbf{s}'$, then **C** is executed again, but this time in $\mathbf{s}'[2/\iota]$, and then control passes to the rest of the program **c**.

11. Own-variables

In this chapter we discuss the semantics of ALGOL 60 own-variables. Since most people feel that these are badly designed, we need to explain why it is worth considering their semantics at all. The two main reasons are:

(i) The semantics of own-variables vividly shows how a construct which is at first sight intuitively clean is in fact very messy and fraught with subtle ambiguities. Thus it illustrates one kind of insight one can rapidly gain by attempting a formal description. It is true that the various ambiguities were discovered without using any formal methods, but their uncovering took several years. Had a formal semantics been attempted, the ambiguities would immediately have revealed themselves and one would have been forced to face and resolve them. Also, semantic concepts enable one to concisely and lucidly articulate all the possible interpretations.

(ii) The semantics of own-variables requires the use of 'position dependent denotations' and the techniques of handling these are of some interest in their own right. Although these techniques are not very often useful for describing the *conceptual meaning* of languages—which is what this book has concentrated on—they are required in describing operational semantics modelling implementations.

The intuitive idea of own-variables is simple: an own-variable is a local variable of a block which 'remembers' its value between activations of the block. Thus if control leaves a block and then some time later re-enters it, the contents of the own-variables on entry are what they were on the preceding exit. A typical use of own-variables is the following ALGOL 60 procedure:

```
integer procedure count;
begin  own integer n;
       count: = n;
       n: = n + 1
end
```

If we assume the own-variable **n** is initialized to **0** (as in modern ALGOL 60) then successive calls of **count** will produce successive integers starting with **0**—i.e. the first time **count** is called it will return **0**, the next time **1**, and so on. Each time **count** exits, the own-variable **n**, though inaccessible, still exists and can be read and updated by entering the block in which it was declared—i.e. by calling **count** again. Before proceeding to the semantics of own-variables, we point out that most of their uses can be better achieved with the much cleaner **within** construct.

11.1 The within construct

If $\mathbf{D}_1$ and $\mathbf{D}_2$ are declarations then $\mathbf{D}_1$ **within** $\mathbf{D}_2$ is a declaration whose meaning is that $\mathbf{D}_1$ is 'local' to $\mathbf{D}_2$—thus $\mathbf{D}_1$ **within** $\mathbf{D}_2$ is like a block whose body is $\mathbf{D}_2$ (perhaps a syntax **begin** $\mathbf{D}_1;\mathbf{D}_2$ **end** would thus have been better). The semantics is simply:

$$\mathcal{D}[\mathrm{D}_1 \textbf{ within } \mathrm{D}_2]\,\mathrm{r}\,\mathrm{u} = \mathcal{D}[\mathrm{D}_1]\,\mathrm{r};\lambda\mathrm{r}'.\,\mathcal{D}[\mathrm{D}_2]\,\mathrm{r}[\mathrm{r}']\,\mathrm{u}$$

Using the within construct, the function **count** can be elegantly programmed by:

var n = **0 within (integer procedure** count;count: = n;n: = n + **1)**

11.2. Different interpretations of ALGOL 60 own-variables

In early descriptions of ALGOL 60, own-variables were ambiguously described and various rival interpretations arose. These interpretations differ on the times at which own-variables declared in procedure bodies are initialized. We shall consider three possibilities.

(i) The *static* interpretation: all own-variables are initialized before the program containing them is run. Thus own-variables can be thought of as global variables declared in an imaginary outermost block but only 'visible' within the block in which they are declared. This is now the official interpretation.

(ii) The *intermediate* interpretation: own-variables in a procedure body get initialized each time the procedure is *declared.*

(iii) The *dynamic* interpretation: own variable in a procedure body get initialized each time the procedure is *called*.

To illustrate the difference between these interpretations consider the ALGOL 60 program below:

```
begin
      L:begin integerprocedure count;
                          begin   own integer n;
                                  count: = n;
                                  n: = n + 1
                          end
                   print  count;
                   print  count;
        end
        goto  L
end
```

(i) On the static interpretation, **n** is initialized just once to **0** at the beginning, and so the program will loop forever, printing **0**, **1**, **2**, ... (each time **count** is called **n** is increased by **1**).

(ii) On the intermediate interpretation, each time **count** is declared, **n** will be reinitialized to **0**, so the program will loop forever, printing **0**, **1**, **0**, **1**, **0**, **1**, ...

(iii) On the dynamic interpretation, each time **count** is called, **n** will be reinitialized to **0**, so the program will loop forever, printing **0**, **0**, **0**, **0**, ...

11.3. Semantics of own-variables

To show how to formally describe own-variables we add declarations **own I** = **E** to SMALL. When **I** is initialized, it is bound to a new location containing **E**'s R-value. Because of the possibility that the same identifier might be declared to denote different own-variables in different blocks we must somehow arrange that a single identifier can simultaneously denote several own-variables. We shall do this by introducing a domain **Posn** of 'positions' and then redefine environments by

$$\mathbf{Env} = \underbrace{[\mathbf{Ide} \to [\mathbf{Dv} + \{\mathbf{unbound}\}]]}_{\text{ordinary bindings}} \times \underbrace{[[\mathbf{Ide} \times \mathbf{Posn}] \to [\mathbf{Loc} + \{\mathbf{unbound}\}]]}_{\text{own-variable bindings}}$$

The bindings of ordinary variables, constants, procedures, functions, etc., will be held in the first component, which has type **Ide→[Dv + {unbound}]**. In the second component, of type **[Ide × Posn]→[Loc + {unbound}]**, we hold the bindings of own-variables—specifically, if **I** is declared at position **w**ε**Posn** to denote location **ı**, then we bind **ı** to the pair **(I,w)** in the second component. To make this intelligible we must explain **Posn.** Pretty well any way of distinguishing different occurrences of declarations could be used to disambiguate own-variable names. We shall 'name' each occurrence of a construct in a program by its position, which we represent as a string of numbers as follows:

(i) The position of the whole program is the empty string **( )**.

(ii) If a construct has position **w** then its immediate constituents have positions **w.1, w.2, w.3,** ... from left to right.

Thus we define **Posn** = **Num***. As an example, consider the following silly program:

program begin proc P(x); **output** (x + x);
P(1);
P(1)
end

The position of the whole program is **( )**. The position of the block constituting the body of the program is **(1)**. The position of the declaration of **P** is **1.1**. The position of the first call **P(1)** is **1.2**. The position of the second call **P(1)** is **1.3**. The positions of **P**, **x** and **output (x + x)** in the declaration of **P** are **1.1.1**, **1.1.2** and **1.1.3**.

To initialize own-variables we use a function **W** (so named because of the w in own) which when applied to constructs, locates the own-variable declarations in them and generates the appropriate bindings. **W** has type:

$$\mathbf{W}:[\mathbf{Com}+\mathbf{Dec}]\rightarrow\mathbf{Posn}\rightarrow\mathbf{Env}\rightarrow\mathbf{Dc}\rightarrow\mathbf{Cc}$$

and the idea is that

$$\mathbf{W}[\![\mathbf{X}]\!]\,\mathbf{w}\,\mathbf{r}\,\mathbf{u} = \mathbf{u}((\,),(\imath_1,\ldots,\imath_n/(\mathbf{I}_1,\mathbf{w}_1),\ldots,(\mathbf{I}_n,\mathbf{w}_n)))$$

where $\mathbf{I}_1,\ldots,\mathbf{I}_n$ are the identifiers declared to denote own-variables in **X** (**X** is either a command or a declaration) at positions $\mathbf{w}_1,\ldots,\mathbf{w}_n$, and $\imath_1,\ldots,\imath_n$ are new locations initialized appropriately. Thus **W** passes an environment containing an empty—i.e. **()**—normal part and new own-variable bindings to **u**. The definition of **W** is straightforward.

Those constructs which cannot have own-variable declarations hidden in them generate empty bindings. Thus

$$\begin{aligned} \mathbf{W}[\mathrm{I}:=\mathrm{E}]\,\mathbf{w\,r\,u} &= \mathbf{u}((\,),(\,)) \\ \mathbf{W}[\textbf{output}\ \mathrm{E}]\,\mathbf{w\,r\,u} &= \mathbf{u}((\,),(\,)) \\ \mathbf{W}[\mathrm{E}_1(\mathrm{E}_2)]\,\mathbf{w\,r\,u} &= \mathbf{u}((\,),(\,)) \\ \mathbf{W}[\textbf{var}\ \mathrm{I}=\mathrm{E}]\,\mathbf{w\,r\,u} &= \mathbf{u}((\,),(\,)) \end{aligned}$$

The bindings of commands which contain other commands as constituents are got by merging the bindings of the constituents. Thus:

$$\mathbf{W}[\textbf{while}\ \mathrm{E}\ \textbf{do}\ \mathrm{C}]\,\mathbf{w\,r\,u} = \mathbf{W}[\mathrm{C}]\,\mathbf{w.2\,r\,u}$$

$$\begin{aligned} &\mathbf{W}[\textbf{if}\ \mathrm{E}\ \textbf{then}\ \mathrm{C}_1\ \textbf{else}\ \mathrm{C}_2]\,\mathbf{w\,r\,u} = \\ &\quad \mathbf{W}[\mathrm{C}_1]\,\mathbf{w.2\,r}\,\lambda\mathbf{r}_1\,.\,\mathbf{W}[\mathrm{C}_2]\,\mathbf{w.3\,r}\,\lambda\mathbf{r}_2\,.\,\mathbf{u}(\mathbf{r}_1[\mathbf{r}_2]) \end{aligned}$$

$$\begin{aligned} &\mathbf{W}[\textbf{begin}\ \mathrm{D;C}\ \textbf{end}]\,\mathbf{w\,r\,u} = \\ &\quad \mathbf{W}[\mathrm{D}]\,\mathbf{w.1\,r}\,\lambda\mathbf{r}_1\,.\,\mathbf{W}[\mathrm{C}]\,\mathbf{w.2\,r}\,\lambda\mathbf{r}_2\,.\,\mathbf{u}(\mathbf{r}_1[\mathbf{r}_2]) \end{aligned}$$

$$\begin{aligned} &\mathbf{W}[\mathrm{C}_1;\mathrm{C}_2]\,\mathbf{w\,r\,u} = \\ &\quad \mathbf{W}[\mathrm{C}_1]\,\mathbf{w.1\,r}\,\lambda\mathbf{r}_1\,.\,\mathbf{W}[\mathrm{C}_2]\,\mathbf{w.2\,r}\,\lambda\mathbf{r}_2\,.\,\mathbf{u}(\mathbf{r}_1[\mathbf{r}_2]) \end{aligned}$$

Here $\mathbf{r}_1[\mathbf{r}_2]$ means the environment obtained by merging the normal part of $\mathbf{r}_1$ with the normal part of $\mathbf{r}_2$ and the own-variable part of $\mathbf{r}_1$ with that of $\mathbf{r}_2$. Notice how we 'pass down' the appropriate position to each constituent; this ensures that we can generate different bindings for the same identifier declared own in different positions. The clause which actually generates these bindings is:

$$\mathbf{W}[\textbf{own}\ \mathrm{I}=\mathrm{E}]\,\mathbf{w\,r\,u} = \mathbf{R}[\mathrm{E}]\,\mathbf{r;ref}\,\lambda\iota\,.\,\mathbf{u}((\,),(\iota/(\mathrm{I},\mathbf{w})))$$

Finally, we must define **W**[**proc** I(I_1);C]. If own-variables in procedure bodies are initialized at the same time as all other own-variables, i.e. before the program has been run, then:

$$\mathbf{W}[\textbf{proc}\ \mathrm{I}(\mathrm{I}_1);\mathrm{C}]\,\mathbf{w\,r\,u} = \mathbf{W}[\mathrm{C}]\,\mathbf{w.3\,r\,u}$$

This corresponds to the static interpretation. With the other interpretations, the own-variables in **C** are not initialized at the beginning, and so

$$\mathbf{W}[\textbf{proc}\ \mathrm{I}(\mathrm{I}_1);\mathrm{C}]\,\mathbf{w\,r\,u} = \mathbf{u}((\,),(\,))$$

In this case the semantic clause for **D[proc I(I_1);C]** must ensure that initialization is done at the right time. With the intermediate interpretation, initialization is done at declaration time, so, if **w** is the position of **C**, then we need something like:

$$\mathbf{D[proc\ I(I_1);C]\ r\ u = W[C]\ w\ r\ \lambda r'.\ u((p/I),(\,))}$$
$$\mathbf{where\ p = \lambda c\ e\ .\ C[C]\ r[r'][e/I_1]\ c}$$

Here, at declaration time we generate an initialization **r′** of the own-variables in the body **C** and bind that into the procedure value. This semantic clause is defective in various ways which we rectify below—first, though, we give a defective clause for the dynamic interpretation. With this, the initialization is done each time the procedure is called, so each time the procedure value **p** is applied it must invoke **W**. Thus

$$\mathbf{D[proc\ I(I_1);C]\ r\ u = u((p/I),(\,))}$$
$$\mathbf{where\ p = \lambda c\ e\ .\ W[C]\ w\ r[e/I_1]\ \lambda r'\ .\ C[C]\ r[r'][e/I_1]\ c}$$

so **r′** is generated each time the procedure is called. The last two clauses are defective because the position **w** occurring in their right hand sides is not defined. What we must do is change **C** and **D** so that they 'pass positions down' to their constituents. (The problem we are having with **w** is like the problem we had with **valof** continuations **k** discussed in 7.1.3.—we adopt the analogue of solution (i) to handle **w**.) Thus we must change the types of **C** and **D** so that

$$\mathbf{C{:}Com \to Posn \to Env \to Cc \to Cc}$$
$$\mathbf{D{:}Dec \to Posn \to Env \to Dc \to Cc}$$

The semantic clauses must now be rewritten to handle:

(i) The passing down of positions.
(ii) The new environments.
(iii) The binding of own-variables to their names in their scopes.

To cope with (i) we proceed as in the definition of **W**, for example

$$\mathbf{C[if\ E\ then\ C_1\ else\ C_2]\ w\ r\ c =}$$
$$\mathbf{R[E]\ r;Bool?;cond(C[C_1]\ w.2\ r\ c\ ,\ C[C_2]\ w.3\ r\ c)}$$

N.B. (arrows pointing to w.2 and w.3)

$$\mathbf{C}[C_1;C_2]\,w\,r\,c = \mathbf{C}[C_1]\,w.1\,r;\mathbf{C}[C_2]\,w.2\,r;c$$

N.B. (pointing to $w.1$ and $w.2$)

To cope with (ii) we must change $\mathbf{E}[I]$ so that

$$\mathbf{E}[I]\,r\,k = (el\,1\,r\,I = unbound) \rightarrow k(el\,1\,r\,I), err$$

and declarations must generate bindings in the normal part of the environment, thus:

$$\begin{aligned} \mathbf{D}[\mathbf{const}\ I = E]\,w\,r\,u &= \mathbf{R}[E]\,r\,\lambda e\,.\,u((e/I),(\,)) \\ \mathbf{D}[\mathbf{var}\ I = E]\,w\,r\,u &= \mathbf{R}[E]\,r;ref\,\lambda\iota\,.\,u((\iota/I),(\,)) \end{aligned}$$

For procedure and function declarations we require a different semantic clause for each interpretation of own-variables, these clauses being the correct versions of the defective ones discussed above. We just give the clauses for procedures, as the ones for functions are similar.

11.3.1. Static interpretation

$$\begin{aligned} \mathbf{D}[\mathbf{proc}\ I(I_1);C]\,w\,r\,u &= u((p/I),(\,)) \\ \text{where } p &= \lambda c\,e\,.\,\mathbf{C}[C]\,w.3\,r[e/I_1]\,c \end{aligned}$$

No initialization is done at either declaration or call time—it is all done before the program is run.

11.3.2. Intermediate interpretation

$$\begin{aligned} \mathbf{D}[\mathbf{proc}\ I(I_1);C]\,w\,r\,u &= \mathbf{W}[C]\,w.3\,r\,\lambda r'\,.\,u((p/I),(\,)) \\ \text{where } p &= \lambda c\,e\,.\,\mathbf{C}[C]\,w.3\,r[r'][e/I_1]\,c \end{aligned}$$

Initialization is done at declaration time.

11.3.3. Dynamic interpretation

$$\begin{aligned} \mathbf{D}[\mathbf{proc}\ I(I_1);C]\,w\,r\,u &= u((p/I),(\,)) \\ \text{where } p &= \lambda c\,e\,.\,\mathbf{W}[C]\,w.3\,r[e/I]\,\lambda r'\,.\,\mathbf{C}[C]\,w.3\,r[r'][e/I_1]\,c \end{aligned}$$

Initialization is done at call time.

Notice that with the dynamic interpretation procedures like

proc P(x);**begin own** I = x;...**end**

make sense. With the static or intermediate interpretation the **x** in **own I = x** would be evaluated in the initial (i.e. 'compile-time') or declaration-time environments respectively.

We still have not explained how own-variables are made accessible within their scope. This is done by 'moving' the bindings from the own-variable part of the environment to the normal part at block entry—i.e. when **own I = E** is executed. Thus

D[own I = E] w r u =
(el 2 r (I,w) = unbound→err , u(((el 2 r (I,w))/I),( )))

so on block entry **E** is ignored (it was evaluated earlier by **W** at 'own-variable initialization time') and the value bound to **(I,w)** in the second component of the environment is bound to **I** in the first component.

Finally, we must fix the semantics **P[P]** of whole programs to initialize own-variables before running the program **P** (with the intermediate or dynamic interpretations, only own-variables not occurring in procedure bodies are initialized now). The position of the 'main command' is **1**; hence:

P[program C] i = W[C] 1 ( ) (λr . C[C] 1 r (λs . stop)) (i/input)

12. Types

In many programming languages, one must declare the *type* of each identifier in use. For example, in PASCAL, variables are declared by: **var I:T,** where **T** is a type such as **integer**, **real**, **array** [1...100] **of real,** etc. The purposes of such explicit types include making programs easier to read; aiding 'debugging' by enabling type errors (such as **1 + true**) to be detected before programs are run; and permitting efficient code to be compiled (by removing the need to generate time-consuming run-time type checks).

To describe the type system of a language one must:

(i) Define what the types are.
(ii) Define which programs are well typed.
(iii) Define how the types relate to the semantic domains.

We consider these in turn in the next three sections.

12.1. Various kinds of types

Both the types available and the nature of the types themselves differ from language to language. For PASCAL, we might use a domain **Type** of types **T** defined by:

$$\begin{aligned} \mathbf{T} ::= \; & \mathbf{integer} \mid \mathbf{real} \mid \mathbf{boolean} \mid \mathbf{char} \mid \\ & \mid \mathbf{B_1 \,..\, B_2} \mid \mathbf{array}\ \mathbf{T_1}\ \mathbf{of}\ \mathbf{T_2} \mid \mathbf{record}\ \mathbf{I_1{:}T_1;\ldots;I_nT_n} \\ & \mid \mathbf{set\ of\ T} \mid \mathbf{file\ of\ T} \mid \ldots \end{aligned}$$

ALGOL 60, on the other hand, has no records, sets or files and its array types do not have any index-type specified. Since ALGOL 60 array bounds are computed dynamically (when the array declaration is executed at run-time) it has array types of the form **T array** (e.g. **integer array**) rather than of the form **array** $\mathbf{T_1}$ **of** $\mathbf{T_2}$ (e.g. **array 1 . . 100 of integer**). Exactly what types are good to have is a current research problem. For instance a number of recent experimental languages allow types to contain *type variables,* so that, for example, a general purpose sorting procedure can take an argument of type **x array** (where **x** is a type variable)— thus avoiding having to write separate procedures for sorting integer arrays, real arrays, ... etc. as one would in ALGOL 60 or PASCAL.

12.2. Well-typed programs and type-checking

Given the types of a language, one must next define which programs are *well-typed.* For example if **x**, **y** have types **integer** and **real** respectively then one must say whether **x + y** is well-typed, and if so what its type is. The process of checking that constructs are well-typed is called *type-checking* and it is important that what has to be checked is carefully specified. There is a notorious ambiguity in the description of which PASCAL programs are well-typed [Welsh, Sneeringer and Hoare]: consider types $\mathbf{T}_1$, $\mathbf{T}_2$ and $\mathbf{T}_3$ defined by:

type $\mathbf{T}_1, \mathbf{T}_2$ = **array 1 . . 100 of integer;**
type $\mathbf{T}_3$ = **array 1 . . 100 of integer**

then it is not clear if $\mathbf{T}_1$ and $\mathbf{T}_2$ are the same type, and if so, whether they are different from $\mathbf{T}_3$. Thus if we declare

var $\mathbf{A}_1$:$\mathbf{T}_1$;
var $\mathbf{A}_2$:$\mathbf{T}_2$;
var $\mathbf{A}_3$:$\mathbf{T}_3$;
procedure P(var x:$\mathbf{T}_1$**);...**

then it is not clear (and is currently implementation-dependent) whether $\mathbf{P(A_2)}$ and $\mathbf{P(A_3)}$ are allowable procedure calls. To settle ambiguities like this the well-typing conditions should be rigorously defined.

Type-checking is at first sight a purely 'syntactic' process; however it is possible—at least for simple languages—to describe it denotationally. The idea is that one regards programs as having two sets of meanings: a 'dynamic meaning' which describes their execution, and a 'static meaning' which describes their type-checking. Looked at this way, types are 'static values' computed (usually) at compile-time. Thus, just as at run-time **2 + 3.5** evaluates to **5.5,** so at compile-time, **integer + real** evaluates to **real**. Thus type-checking is thought of as a 'non-standard' model of the language in which calculations with types replace calculations with (run-time) values. This approach appears elegant and unifying and it works well for simple type systems (as found in FORTRAN, ALGOL 60, ALGOL 68, PASCAL etc.); we outline the details in the next section. However for more sophisticated systems—for example, those which use type variables—it may be conceptually confusing and technically inefficient. Since this is still a research area, we shall not attempt further discussion.

12.2.1. The denotational description of type-checking (outline)

Describing type-checking denotationally is just like describing run-time meanings, but much easier. For example, we might define a domain **Tenv** of *type environments* by:

$$\mathbf{Tenv} = \mathbf{Ide} \rightarrow [\mathbf{Type} + \{\mathbf{unbound}\}]$$

A type environment **r** specifies the types of the various identifiers in the program. We might then define static semantic functions

$$\mathbf{ET}: \mathbf{Exp} \rightarrow \mathbf{Tenv} \rightarrow [\mathbf{Type} + \{\mathbf{typeerror}\}]$$
$$\mathbf{CT}: \mathbf{Com} \rightarrow \mathbf{Tenv} \rightarrow \{\mathbf{welltyped}, \mathbf{typeerror}\}$$
$$\mathbf{DT}: \mathbf{Dec} \rightarrow \mathbf{Tenv} \rightarrow [\mathbf{Tenv} + \{\mathbf{typeerror}\}]$$

where intuitively:

$$\mathbf{ET}[\mathbf{E}]\,\mathbf{r} = \begin{cases} \mathbf{T} & \text{if } \mathbf{E} \text{ is well-typed and has type } \mathbf{T} \text{ in } \mathbf{r} \\ \mathbf{typeerror} & \text{if } \mathbf{E} \text{ is badly typed} \end{cases}$$

$$\mathbf{CT}[\mathbf{C}]\,\mathbf{r} = \begin{cases} \mathbf{welltyped} & \text{if } \mathbf{C} \text{ is well-typed} \\ \mathbf{typeerror} & \text{if } \mathbf{C} \text{ is badly typed} \end{cases}$$

$$\mathbf{DT}[\mathbf{D}]\,\mathbf{r} = \begin{cases} \mathbf{r}' & \text{if } \mathbf{D} \text{ is well-typed and } \mathbf{r}' \text{ gives the types} \\ & \quad \text{of the identifiers declared in } \mathbf{D} \\ \mathbf{typeerror} & \text{if } \mathbf{D} \text{ is badly typed} \end{cases}$$

Typical 'static' semantic clauses would be:

$$\mathbf{ET}[\mathbf{true}]\,\mathbf{r} = \mathbf{boolean}$$
$$\mathbf{ET}[\mathbf{I}]\,\mathbf{r} = (\mathbf{r}\,\mathbf{I} = \mathbf{unbound}) \rightarrow \mathbf{typeerror}\,,\, \mathbf{r}\,\mathbf{I}$$
$$\mathbf{ET}[\mathbf{E}_1[\mathbf{E}_2]]\,\mathbf{r} =$$
$$\quad (\mathbf{ET}[\mathbf{E}_1]\,\mathbf{r} = \mathbf{array}\ \mathbf{T}_1\ \mathbf{of}\ \mathbf{T}_2)\ \mathbf{and}\ (\mathbf{ET}[\mathbf{E}_2]\,\mathbf{r} = \mathbf{T}_1) \rightarrow \mathbf{T}_2\,,\, \mathbf{typeerror}$$
$$\mathbf{CT}[\mathbf{if}\ \mathbf{E}\ \mathbf{then}\ \mathbf{C}_1\ \mathbf{else}\ \mathbf{C}_2]\,\mathbf{r} =$$
$$\quad (\mathbf{ET}[\mathbf{E}]\,\mathbf{r} = \mathbf{boolean}) \rightarrow$$
$$\quad ((\mathbf{CT}[\mathbf{C}_1]\,\mathbf{r} = \mathbf{CT}[\mathbf{C}_2]\,\mathbf{r} = \mathbf{welltyped}) \rightarrow \mathbf{welltyped},\, \mathbf{typeerror}),$$
$$\qquad \mathbf{typeerror}$$
$$\mathbf{DT}[\mathbf{const}\ \mathbf{I}{:}\mathbf{T} = \mathbf{E}]\,\mathbf{r} = (\mathbf{ET}[\mathbf{E}]\,\mathbf{r} = \mathbf{T}) \rightarrow (\mathbf{T}/\mathbf{I})\,,\, \mathbf{typeerror}$$

(Here we assume PASCAL-style arrays, and constant declarations **const I:T = E** where **I** is declared to have type **T** and is initialized (at run-time) to **E**'s value). We shall not give a fully worked out example since for simple type systems, the details are very straightforward, and for complex systems they are unclear.

12.3. The semantics of types

To fully explain the types of a language one must relate them to the (run-time) semantic domains. For example, if **I** is declared to be a variable of type **integer,** then this means that only members of the semantic domain **Num** (say) should be stored in it. Having defined the *meaning* of types, one can then *prove* that well-typed programs conform to this meaning. For example, one could attempt to prove that if **ET[E] r = integer** then **E** (the run-time semantic function) gives a member of **Num** as **E**'s value. Whether or not this is true depends on whether the language has a *secure* type system. This question—whether programs which are *syntactically* well-typed (i.e. successfully type-checked) are always *semantically* well-typed (i.e. do not cause run-time type errors)—is thus an important question to ask when designing a language. Both ALGOL 60 and PASCAL have needless type insecurities illustrated by the following PASCAL program [Welsh, Sneeringer and Hoare]:

```
procedure P(procedure Q);begin Q(1,2) end;
procedure R(x:integer);begin write (x) end;
begin P(R) end
```

Since one cannot say that **Q** must take two parameters, there is no way to exclude **P** being applied to **R**, which only takes one. Had the designers thought about proving that well-typed programs cannot cause run-time type errors, then perhaps they would have avoided this—say by requiring one to write:

```
procedure P(procedure Q (integer,integer));...
```

Unfortunately there are as yet unanswered technical difficulties in giving the semantics of all except the most trivial types. Intuitively one would like to define a semantic function, **T** say, such that

T:Type→{denotations of types}

where the denotation of a type **T** is something like the *set of values* having type **T**. Thus we might define **Tv** by:

$$\mathbf{Tv} = \{\mathbf{x} \mid \mathbf{x} \text{ is a subset of } \mathbf{Ev}\}$$

and then $\mathbf{T}$:**Type**→**Tv** might be defined by:

$$\begin{aligned} \mathbf{T[integer]} &= \{\mathbf{e} \mid \mathbf{isNum\ e = true}\} \\ \mathbf{T[boolean]} &= \{\mathbf{e} \mid \mathbf{isBool\ e = true}\} \\ &\vdots \end{aligned}$$

Alas, there appear to be technical problems with this, and it is not clear if such an approach is mathematically sound. We cannot go into the details here, but interested readers could look at [Donahue] and [Reynolds].

Appendix: Remarks for instructors and sample exercises

This book is based on a course taught at Edinburgh University to undergraduates and first year graduate students. The material is covered in twelve hour-long lectures over a period of six weeks. Exercises are handed out weekly. At first, the exercises are mainly concerned with using formal notation—especially λ-notation. Students are often confused over the difference between mathematical functions and programs, and they find higher-order functions especially hard to grasp. A typical first exercise sheet would contain questions like Q1 and Q2 below.

The next big problem is getting across how continuations work. From the student's point of view, a good kind of exercise is 'evaluating' particular programs from semantic clauses—e.g. Q4—unfortunately such exercises generate solutions which are very tedious to mark! Exercises like Q3, Q6-Q10 are also good for inducing an understanding of continuations. After the use of the formalism has been mastered, questions can be set on applying it to new constructs. Easy questions of this type are Q6-Q10; harder examples are Q11 and Q12.

Initially, semantic clauses produced by students are often syntactically and semantically ill-formed. Common mistakes are:

(i) To fail to formalize crucial details, and to revert to English when the going gets tough. For example, Q9 might elicit the following:

C[exit] r c = **c′** where **c′** is continuation corresponding to the smallest enclosing **cycle C repeat**.

This is an intuitive description of a semantic clause—the whole problem is to construct an actual clause meeting the description.

(ii) To write semantic clauses which are mathematical rubbish but, in some loose intuitive sense, match a correct informal description, e.g.:

$$\mathbf{O[+](e_1,e_2)\,k = e_1;Num?;e_2;Num?;k(e_1+e_2)}$$

This looks plausible until one considers the types. Q3 is designed to correct this kind of mistake.

(iii) To use various undefined entities, e.g.

D[newvar I] r u = u(new s/I)

Here it is incorrectly assumed that **s**, like a global variable in programming, is floating around in the context.

Finally it is useful to test that all the ideas have fitted together by requiring students to construct the complete semantics of a whole language. Suitable examples can easily be invented by modifying the various constructs in SMALL. Unfortunately, existing 'real' languages, although usually straightforward, are very tedious to describe formally, and are not suitable for (undergraduate) exercises (though they might be good as term projects). Simplified subsets of real languages are more useful for learning basic principles.

Sample exercises

(Q1) Write down the types of the following functions:

(i) $\lambda x . x+1$
(ii) $\lambda(x,y) . x+y$
(iii) $\lambda x\, y . x+y$
(iv) $\lambda f\, x . (f\, x)+1$

(Q2) The function **lit** (list iterator) is defined informally by:

$$\textbf{lit}\, f\, (x_1,\ldots,x_n)\, x_{n+1} = f\, x_1\, (f\, x_2(\ldots(f\, x_n\, x_{n+1})\ldots))$$

For example, if **plusc** = $\lambda x\, y \,.\, x + y$ then:

$$\textbf{lit plusc}\, (x_1,\ldots,x_n)\, x_{n+1} = x_1 + x_2 + \ldots + x_n + x_{n+1}$$

(e.g. **lit plusc (1,2,3) 4 = 10**)

(i) Write down the generic type of **lit**.
(ii) Use λ-notation and recursion (and no elipsis—i.e. "...") to define **lit**.
(iii) Devise a function **f** such that

$$\textbf{lit}\, f\, (x_1,\ldots,x_n)\, x = \begin{cases} \textbf{true} & \text{if } x = x_i \text{ for some } i \\ \textbf{false} & \text{otherwise} \end{cases}$$

(Q3) If $k \varepsilon Ec$ what is the type of:

$$\lambda(e_1,e_2) . \text{isNum}\, e_1 \text{ and isNum}\, e_2 \rightarrow k(e_1 + e_2)\, ,\, \text{err}$$

Show that this function is the same as:

$$\lambda(e_1,e_2) . (\text{Num?}\, \lambda e_1' . (\text{Num?}\, \lambda e_2' . k(e_1' + e_2'))\, e_2)\, e_1$$

(Q4) Use the semantic clauses of SMALL to evaluate

(i) **P[program output 1;output 2] ( )**
(ii) **P[program output (read + read)] 1 . 2**
(iii) **P[program begin var x = read;output x end] ( )**

(Q5) Compare and contrast the following SMALL commands:

(i) **begin const I = E;C end**
(ii) **(pr I;C)(E)**
(iii) **begin proc I′(I);C;I′(E) end**

(Q6) Devise a declaration **dec I = E** so that **begin dec I = E;C end** is completely equivalent to **(pr I;C)(E)**. Demonstrate the equivalence from your semantic clause for **dec I = E**.

(Q7) Describe the semantics of a command **skip** whose execution has no effect. Show that:

(i) $\mathcal{C}$**[C;skip]** = $\mathcal{C}$**[skip;C]** = $\mathcal{C}$**[C]**
(ii) $\mathcal{C}$**[while E do C]** =
$\mathcal{C}$**[if E then (C;while E do C) else skip]**

(Q8) Describe the semantics of a command **stop** whose execution causes the program to stop. Show that $\mathbf{C_1}$**;stop;**$\mathbf{C_2}$ is equivalent to just $\mathbf{C_1}$**;stop**.

(Q9) Describe the semantics of commands **cycle C repeat**, **exit** and **continue** where:

(i) Executing **cycle C repeat** consists of repeatedly executing **C** until an **exit** is encountered, whereupon the loop terminates and control passes to the rest of the program following it.
(ii) Executing **continue** causes a jump to the beginning of the **C** of the smallest enclosing **cycle C repeat**.
(iii) Executing **exit** or **continue** when not in the **C** of a **cycle C repeat** causes an error.

(Q10) Describe the semantics of commands **return** and **result = E** where:

(i) Executing **return** causes a return from the smallest currently entered procedure.
(ii) Executing **result = E** causes a return with **E**'s value from the smallest currently entered function.
(iii) Executing **return** or **result = E** when not in a procedure or function respectively causes an error.

(Q11) Describe how to add ALGOL 60 switches to SMALL. You should proceed as follows:

(i) Read 3.5. and 5.3. of the "Modified Report on the Algorithmic Language ALGOL 60" [Backus *et al.*].
(ii) Devise an abstract syntax for the constructs involved (e.g. switch declarations and designational expressions).
(iii) Decide what new domains (if any) and changes to existing ones are required.
(iv) Write semantic clauses for the various constructs.

(Q12) Describe how to add coroutines to SMALL. Assume a coroutine named **I** is declared by **coroutine I(I_1);C**. To run **I** with actual parameter **E**, one evaluates the expression **run I(E)**. To *temporarily* leave a coroutine one executes the command **leavewith E;** this passes **E**'s value to the context which ran (or resumed) the coroutine. A temporarily-left coroutine can be resumed by evaluating the expression **resume I;** this 'starts up' **I** at the beginning of the command following the last **leavewith E** in **I.** To permanently leave a coroutine one evaluates the expression **quitwith E**; subsequent attempts to resume it cause errors. For example:

```
begin coroutine count (n);
                  while n<3 do
                    (leavewith n;
                      n: = n + 1);
                  quitwith 3;
      output run count (0);    —outputs 0 and leaves
      output resume count;  —outputs 1 and leaves
      output resume count;  —outputs 2 and leaves
      output resume count;  —outputs 3 and quits
      output resume count;  —causes an error
end
```

References

Extensive bibliographies can be found in [Scott] and [Stoy]; here we just list the references mentioned in the text.

Backus, J. W., *et al.*: *Modified Report on the Algorithmic Language ALGOL 60;* The Computer Journal Vol. 19, No. 4 (1976)

Bjorner, D., and Jones, C.: *The Vienna Development Method: The Meta-Language;* Vol. 61, Lecture Notes in Computer Science, Springer-Verlag (1978)

Burstall, R. M., *et al.*: *Programming in POP-2;* Edinburgh University Press (1971)

Donahue, J.: *On the Semantics of "Data Type";* TR 77-311, Computer Science Department, Cornell University (1977)

Evans, A.: *PAL Reference Manual and Primer;* Department of Electrical Engineering, MIT (1970)

Hanson, D. R.: *The Syntax and Semantics of SL5;* SL5 Project Document S5LD2b, The University of Arizona, Tucson, Arizona (1976)

Jensen, K., and Wirth, N.: *PASCAL User Manual and Report;* Springer-Verlag (1974)

Knuth, D. E. *The Remaining Trouble Spots in ALGOL 60;* Communications of the ACM, Vol. 10, No. 10 (1967)

Knuth, D. E.: *Structured Programming with GOTO Statements;* STAN-CS-74-416, Computer Science Department, Stanford University (1974)

Landin, P. J.: *A Correspondence between ALGOL 60 and Church's Lambda-Notation;* Communications of the ACM, Vol. 8, Nos. 2, 3 (1965)

Ligler, G.T.: *A Mathematical Approach to Language Design;* Proceedings of the Second ACM Symposium on Principles of Programming Languages, Palo Alto (1975)

London, R. L., *et al.*: *Proof Rules for the Programming Language Euclid;* Acta Informatica, Vol. 10, No. 1 (1978)

McCarthy, J.: *A Formal Description of a Subset of ALGOL*, pp. 1-7 of *Formal Language Description Languages for Computer Programming* (ed. Steel, T. B.), North Holland (1966)

Milne, G. J., and Milner, A. J. R. G.: *Concurrent Processes and their Syntax;* Journal of the ACM (1979)

Milne, R. E., and Strachey, C.: *A Theory of Programming Language Semantics;* Chapman and Hall (UK), John Wiley (USA) (1976)

Milner, A. J. R. G.: *Processes: A Mathematical Model of Computing Agents;* pp. 157-174 of the Proceeding of the Logic Colloquim '73 (ed. Rose, H. E., and Shepherdson, J. C.), North Holland (1975)

Mosses, P. D.: *Compiler Generation Using Denotational Semantics;* pp. 436-441 of *Mathematical Foundations of Computer Science*, Gdansk, Lecture Notes in Computer Science, Vol. 45, Springer-Verlag (1976)

Reynolds, J. C.: *Towards a Theory of Type Structure;* Colloquium on Programming, Paris (1974)

Scott, D. S.: *Data Types as Lattices;* SIAM Journal of Computing, Vol. 5, No. 3 (1976)

Stoy, J. E.: *Denotational Semantics: The Scott-Strachey Approach to Programming Language Theory*. MIT Press (1977)

Strachey, C.: *Towards a Formal Semantics;* pp. 198-220 of *Formal Language Description Languages for Computer Programming* (ed. Steel, T. B.), North Holland (1966)

Strachey, C.: *The Varieties of Programming Languages;* Proceedings of the International Computing Symposium, Cini Foundation, Venice (1972) and PRG-10 Programming Research Group, University of Oxford (1974)

Strachey, C., and Wadsworth, C. P.: *Continuations—a Mathematical Semantics for Handling Full Jumps;* PRG-11, Programming Research Group, University of Oxford (1974)

Tennent, R. D.: *Language Design Methods Based on Semantic Principles;* Acta Informatica 8 (1977)

Welsh, J., Sneeringer, W. J., and, Hoare, C. A. R.: *Ambiguities and Insecurities in PASCAL;* Software Practice and Experience 7 (1977)

Zahn, C. T.: *A Control Statement for Natural Top-Down Structured Programming;* Symposium on Programming Languages, Paris (1975)

Subject and Author Index

Symbols